# MODERN
# FARM BUILDINGS:
## THEIR CONSTRUCTION & ARRANGEMENT.

BY

## A. DUDLEY CLARKE, F.S.I.,
LAND AGENT,
SILVER MEDALLIST OF THE ROYAL AGRICULTURAL SOCIETY FOR PLANS OF
FARM BUILDINGS.

*THIRD EDITION, REVISED AND ENLARGED.*

---

"The designing and erection of farm buildings has become one of the most important branches of estate management; the skill and ability displayed in their arrangement and construction exercises an effect on the progress of agriculture measured—not by a lifetime—but by centuries."—"ICH DIEN" in *Agricultural Gazette.*

---

Copyright © 2013 Read Books Ltd.
This book is copyright and may not be
reproduced or copied in any way without
the express permission of the publisher in writing

British Library Cataloguing-in-Publication Data
A catalogue record for this book is available from the
British Library

# Farming

Agriculture, also called farming or husbandry, is the cultivation of animals, plants, or fungi for fibre, biofuel, drugs and other products used to sustain and enhance human life. Agriculture was the key development in the rise of sedentary human civilization, whereby farming of domesticated species created food surpluses that nurtured the development of civilization. It is hence, of extraordinary importance for the development of society, as we know it today. The word *agriculture* is a late Middle English adaptation of Latin *agricultūra*, from *ager*, 'field', and *cultūra*, 'cultivation' or 'growing'. The history of agriculture dates back thousands of years, and its development has been driven and defined by vastly different climates, cultures, and technologies. However all farming generally relies on techniques to expand and maintain the lands that are suitable for raising domesticated species. For plants, this usually requires some form of irrigation, although there are methods of dryland farming. Livestock are raised in a combination of grassland-based and landless systems, in an industry that covers almost one-third of the world's ice- and water-free area.

Agricultural practices such as irrigation, crop rotation, fertilizers, pesticides and the domestication of livestock were developed long ago, but have made great progress in the past century. The history of agriculture has played a major role in human history, as agricultural progress has been a crucial factor in worldwide socio-economic change. Division of labour in agricultural societies made (now) commonplace specializations, rarely seen in hunter-gatherer cultures, which allowed the growth of towns and cities, and the complex societies we call civilizations. When farmers became capable of producing food beyond the needs of their own families, others in their society were freed to devote themselves to projects other than food acquisition. Historians and anthropologists have long argued that the development of agriculture made civilization possible.

In the developed world, industrial agriculture based on large-scale monoculture has become the dominant system of modern farming, although there is growing support for sustainable agriculture, including permaculture and organic agriculture. Until the Industrial Revolution, the vast majority of the human population laboured in agriculture. Pre-industrial agriculture was typically for self-sustenance, in which farmers raised most of their crops for their own consumption, instead of cash crops for trade. A remarkable shift in agricultural practices has occurred over the past two centuries however, in response to new technologies, and the development of world markets. This also has led to technological improvements in agricultural techniques, such as the Haber-Bosch method for synthesizing ammonium nitrate which made the traditional practice of recycling nutrients with crop rotation and animal manure less important.

Modern agronomy, plant breeding, agrochemicals such as pesticides and fertilizers, and technological improvements have sharply increased yields from cultivation, but at the same time have caused widespread ecological damage and negative human health effects. Selective breeding and modern practices in animal husbandry have similarly increased the output of meat, but have raised concerns about animal welfare and the health effects of the antibiotics, growth hormones, and other chemicals commonly used in industrial meat production. Genetically Modified Organisms are an increasing component of agriculture today, although they are banned in several countries. Another controversial issue is 'water management'; an increasingly global issue fostering debate. Significant degradation of land and water resources, including the depletion of aquifers, has been observed in recent decades, and the effects of global warming on agriculture and of agriculture on global warming are still not fully understood.

The agricultural world of today is at a cross roads. Over one third of the worlds workers are employed in agriculture, second only to the services sector, but its future is uncertain. A constantly growing world population is necessitating more and more land being utilised for growth of food stuffs, but also the burgeoning mechanised methods of food cultivation and harvesting means that many farming jobs are becoming redundant. Quite how the sector will respond to these challenges remains to be seen.

# PREFACE TO THE THIRD EDITION.

A THIRD edition of this work having become necessary, the opportunity has been taken of introducing information upon several matters which have recently engaged considerable attention.

The awakening of local authorities to the need for taking greater sanitary precautions against the spreading of tuberculosis and other diseases, by the improved construction and management of cow-houses, raises important issues to landlords and tenants, more particularly where the buildings are situated in populous districts. The various points in connection therewith have been considered, and a reprint is given in the Appendix of the " Model Regulations: Dairies, Cowsheds, and Milkshops," which has been recently issued by the Local Government Board for the guidance of local authorities.

Chapters, with illustrations, have been added on Cottages, Homesteads for Small Holdings, and Iron and Wood Roofs, with a comparison of their cost and respective advantages for farming purposes ; and in response to a suggestion made in a review of the last edition in the *Royal Agricultural Society's Journal* a short chapter on the subject of Repairs and Materials has also been appended.

A. DUDLEY CLARKE.

ABBERLEY, STOURPORT,
*August* 1899.

# PREFACE TO THE SECOND EDITION.

THE fact of a second edition of this handbook having been called for, justifies the hope I expressed in the preface of the first edition that "it would be of some service to those having the charge of landed estates, and to students and pupils who are qualifying themselves for practice," and I gratefully accept the assurance of its serviceability by the Council of the Surveyors' Institution, inasmuch as it is adopted by them as one of the text-books for the Institution examinations.

So short a time having elapsed since the former issue, much revision has not been found necessary; but in view of the financial difficulties which still embarrass the agricultural interests, I have more particularly directed attention to the suitability of corrugated iron for farm buildings, and recommended its more extended use on the score of economy.

A. DUDLEY CLARKE.

ABBERLEY, STOURPORT,
*August* 1895.

# PREFACE TO THE FIRST EDITION.

IT was the remembrance of difficulties encountered, in my early days, in obtaining information of a practical kind, from a land agency point of view, on the subject of the arrangement and construction of farm buildings, which first prompted me to put on record the results of my own experience, gained as it has been by a residence in different parts of the country, and affording me an acquaintance with varied farming and building operations such as present themselves to a resident land agent.

The matter now collected in the following pages will, I trust, be of some service to those having the charge of landed estates, and to students and pupils who are qualifying themselves for practice. It has recently appeared in a series of articles in the *Estate Clerks of Works Journal*, by means of which it was sought to convey, to the heads of the building staff on landed estates, the ideas and methods which prevail in the minds of land agents (if I may be permitted to speak for some at least of them) in the matter of the equipment of farms with suitable buildings for present farming practice. I thought also that it might be of service to them to become better acquainted with the subject from an agriculturist's point of view—as distinct from an architect's or builder's—than their opportunities sometimes afford them. Hence it will be found that much more space is devoted to describing the convenient modes of arrangement and fitting up of the various structures forming a complete homestead, than the art of building and its details,—matters which I have scarcely attempted to deal with, except where I have some special point of utility or service to draw attention to. It must not be supposed that it has been a part of my purpose to recommend an expenditure of money on building improvements, although the advantages of a well-arranged homestead have been pointed out. My remarks are intended more particularly to apply to the *method* of its application where improvements have been found desirable, and to the avoidance of errors which are often made by the inexperienced, to whom I will tender a few words of caution on the subject.

Do not be tempted into the belief that extra good buildings will render more easy to let an indifferent farm. Do not take it for granted that tenants clamouring for new buildings will always be satisfied when they get them—a notice to quit may follow. Be careful to see that any works executed are likely to be valued by succeeding, as well as present tenants ; and avoid, so far as possible, the erection of specialities to meet departures from the ordinary farming practice of the district.

If proof is needed of the necessity for proceeding with caution in the matter of improving and adding to homesteads, one significant fact alone supplies it. This is, that farms are to be found in every district which are let for no higher rent than a sum equal to a moderate interest on the outlay of money made for building the homestead and draining the land.

ABBERLEY, STOURPORT,
*August* 1891.

# CONTENTS.

## CHAPTER I.

PAGE

INTRODUCTION.—Proper arrangement of buildings an assistance to farmers—Good buildings a benefit to landlords—Improvement of homesteads by readaptation of old barns—Buildings should not be too costly, in view of changes in farming practice, and of subdivision into smaller holdings—Necessity for information on farming practice in order to design successfully—Its variation, and influence on the buildings—Ideas of tenants not to be unduly favoured—An out-of-date homestead described—Points requiring consideration for its improvement in arable districts—The same for pastoral districts—Necessity for economising straw by restricting area of yards—Study of farming practice as pursued at homesteads desirable - - 1

## CHAPTER II.

THE ARRANGEMENT OF HOMESTEADS.—Principles of arrangement—Working convenience—Form of arrangement, as a general guide, illustrated by a "text plan" of buildings for an arable farm which received the R.A.S.E. Silver Medal at Kilburn—Description of plan—Description of "Surveyors' Institution" design for buildings for a 400-acre farm, chiefly arable—Method of adapting the foregoing designs to dairy farms, illustrated by plans—Similar features of arrangement embodied in a design for 200 acres of arable—Alterations required for its adoption on a dairy farm - - 10

## CHAPTER III.

THE REMODELLING OF OLD HOMESTEADS.—Points to be considered —How mistakes arise—Farmers with specialities—Plans and descriptions of two old homesteads and barns remodelled—Modern uses to which barns can be applied - - - - - 31

Contents.

## CHAPTER IV.

PAGE

FOOD DEPARTMENT.—Straw, chaff, root, mixing and grain stores—Advantages of the preparation of food—Straw economised thereby, and farmers rendered more independent of seasons—Advantageous sale of straw and purchase of cake—Plan and description of food-stores for a large farm, and method of construction—Position of machinery—House for a portable engine  -  -  -  -  41

## CHAPTER V.

COW-HOUSES.—The various methods of treatment of cows—Beneficial effect of warmth—Sanitary laws as regards cow-houses—Model Regulations by the Local Government Board, 1899, thereon—Circular of the Royal Agricultural Society, 1899, thereon—Cubical area per cow in urban districts—Plans of a single and two double cow-houses described, with their proper dimensions—Saving effected by adopting the double cow-house—Section of roof for same—Paving, draining, lighting, and ventilation considered—Railway sleeper and other wood floors—Opinions at the Surveyors' Institution thereon—Section of surface drain—Illustration of best form of window for farm use generally—Mangers and stall divisions illustrated—Loose boxes and calf-houses illustrated—Sparred flooring for calves—Section of calf-house—Necessity for a dry floor for calves  -  -  -  -  -  -  -  49

## CHAPTER VI.

FEEDING STALLS AND BOXES.—Feeding cattle in stalls, boxes, and yards considered, as regards cost of buildings, &c.—Advantage of boxes as regards manure—Plan and section of cattle boxes—Divisions made removable for getting out manure, and for forming a covered yard for young stock—Fitting up of boxes  -  -  72

## CHAPTER VII.

OPEN STOCKYARDS.—Stockyards frequently too large—Area required for each beast—Proportion required to be covered in—Plan of yards with feeding and shelter sheds—Cheap roof to protect mangers—Requirements of good yards—Gates—Walls—Compactness of design minimises labour in attendance  -  -  -  -  77

## Contents.

### CHAPTER VIII.

COVERED YARDS.—Results of the competition in farm building designs at the R.A.S.E. Kilburn Show as regards covered yards—Opinions of the Judges thereon—Remarks on covered yards at the Surveyors' Institution—Their alternative uses—Material points of construction considered—Illustrations of methods of roofing—Cost per yard of corrugated iron roofs—Drainage scarcely necessary—Dr Cameron on the philosophy of sheltering animals as a means of avoiding a wasteful expenditure of heat  -  -  -  -  -  83

### CHAPTER IX.

STABLES.—Opposed practices in the treatment of farm horses—Best position for stables—Dimensions of the building—Boxes—Illustrations of single and double stables—Hay, chaff, and harness rooms—Question of a loft above stables considered—Windows—Ventilation—Flooring materials—Stall divisions—Mangers—Racks, high and low—Desirability of the adoption of fittings which a village tradesman can deal with in the repair stage  -  -  -  94

### CHAPTER X.

PIGGERIES.—Pigs cleanly, and fond of comfort—Warmth necessary for profitable development—Disadvantages of the usual low sty and yard — Box form of sty recommended — Its alternative uses — Flooring—Feeding troughs—Sparred flooring—Food-house and its fittings—Advantages of a warm meal  -  -  -  -  106

### CHAPTER XI.

CART-SHEDDING AND MISCELLANEOUS BUILDINGS.—*Cart-shedding:*—Its situation and aspect—Dimensions—Lean-to structures for small implements—Lock-up place for drills—Tool-house.  *Carpenter's and blacksmith's shops:*—Their advantages—Blacksmith's hearth and fittings.  *Sick boxes and slaughter-houses:*—Considered as extras—Advantages of facilities for killing and dressing animals—Isolation in cases of sickness desirable.  *Manure tanks and drainage:*—Tanks not recommended owing to their non-use—Opinions at the Surveyors' Institution, with alternative proposals for dealing with liquid manure—Mode of constructing tank—A useful pump.  *Water supply:*—Ponds—Pumps—Springs—Pure water necessary for sanitary considerations in dairy—Advantages of

xii                     *Contents.*

obtaining water by gravitation away from all sources of pollution—Cost of same—Hydraulic rams—Supply for troughs and mangers—To movable mangers by a standpipe—To milk cooler - - 112

### CHAPTER XII.

DUTCH BARN AND OTHER ROOFING.—General remarks upon—Iron *versus* wood roofs—Section of curved iron roofs—Method of construction of—Detail drawing of—Cost of iron roof, detailed—Section of wood roofs—Method of construction of—Specification of—Cost of wood roof, detailed—Cost reduced by modifications—Detail of cost of flat iron roofs—Comparative advantages of iron and wood roofs—Their durability—Concluding remarks and suggestions  -  -  -  -  -  -  -  - 125

### CHAPTER XIII.

FARMHOUSES.—Altered domestic life at the farm necessitates various modifications— Requirements influenced by rent rather than by acreage—Accommodation for various rentals from £100 to £500 a year—Site — Drainage — Working apartments — Advantage of improving the elevation of old houses  -  -  -  - 134

### CHAPTER XIV.

HOMESTEADS FOR SMALL HOLDINGS.—Opinion in favour of the extension of small holdings—Cautious procedure recommended—Cause of their disappearance —Some reasons in favour of their reintroduction—Subdivision of farms for, requires discrimination—Points to be considered in connection with the land, houses, and buildings for—Plan and description of farmhouse for £100 a year rental—Plan and description of small farmhouse for 20 to 50 acres—Plans of farm buildings for the same, with specification and description—Cost of the same  -  -  -  -  - 139

### CHAPTER XV.

COTTAGES.—The provision of unremunerative, but necessary—Amount of accommodation required—Advantages of a well-arranged design for—Plan of pair of labourers' cottages with three bedrooms—Plan can be modified and adapted for special requirements—The reduction in size for two bedrooms only—Desirability of providing comfortable cottages—Sanitary considerations—Plan also adaptable for small holdings  -  -  -  -  -  -  - 157

*Contents.* xiii

## CHAPTER XVI.

PAGE

DAIRIES.—Dairy methods of more prominence now than hitherto—Necessity for the avoidance of impurities, and control of temperature—Bradford's prize dairies illustrated and described—Their interest and importance—Aspect—Hollow walls—Roofing material—Mode of ventilation—Heating—Drainage—Working appliances—Dairy practice up to date indicated by these designs—Yield of butter affected by temperature      -      -      -      -      -   163

## CHAPTER XVII.

POULTRY HOUSES.—Poultry-keeping profitable on farms—Two plans and a section given as embodying desirable features—Warmth, freedom from molestation, and cleanliness are the chief elements of success—How attained—Laying away, and desertion of the fowl-houses, the result of neglect in this respect—Fitting up the interior   172

## CHAPTER XVIII.

REPAIRS.—Repairs a large outlay on estates — Customs as to — Best mode of execution considered—Advantages of an efficient staff of estate employés for executing — Difficulties connected with the employment of builders—Arrangements with tenants as to repairs—Landlord to put in repair on entry—Discussions on audit day to be avoided—The suitability of various kinds of home timber for repairs considered—Gate repairs—Cloven gates—Brickmaking in "clamps"      -      -      -      -      -      -      -      -   176

## APPENDIX.

MODEL REGULATIONS.—Dairies, cowsheds, and milkshops   -   -   183

INDEX      -      -      -      -      -      -   183

# LIST OF ILLUSTRATIONS.

|  | PAGE |
|---|---|
| Fig. 1. Plan of Homestead for an Arable Farm of 400 acres | 12 |
| 2. Plan of Homestead for a Farm of 400 acres, one-third pasture | 20 |
| 3. Plan of Homestead for a Dairy Farm of 400 acres and over | 22 |
| 4. Plan of a Homestead for a Dairy Farm of 400 acres | 24 |
| 5. Plan of Homestead for an Arable Farm from 200 to 250 acres | 28 |
| 6. Plan of Old Homestead remodelled (No. 1) | 34 |
| 7. Plan of Old Homestead remodelled (No. 2) | 36 |
| 8. Food Department of Homestead | 42 |
| 9. Single Cow-house | 52 |
| 10. Double Cow-house | 53 |
| 11. Double Cow-house | 54 |
| 12. Section of Roof for Double Cow-house | 55 |
| 13. Section of Cow-house Surface Drain | 60 |
| 14. Elevation of Window | 62 |
| 15. Cow-house Half-pipe Manger | 64 |
| 16. Section of Brick Manger, and Wood Stall Division of Cow-house | 65 |
| 17. Manger of Stoneware Blocks | 66 |
| 18. Plan of Calf-pens attached to Cow-house | 69 |
| 19. Section of Calf-house with Sparred Flooring | 70 |
| 20. Plan of Cattle Boxes | 74 |
| 21. Section of Cattle Boxes | 75 |
| 22. Plan of Stockyards attached to Cow-house or Feeding Stalls | 78 |

## List of Illustrations.

| | | PAGE |
|---|---|---|
| Fig. 23. | Section of Roof over Mangers | 79 |
| 24. | Section of Covered Yard Roof | 90 |
| 25. | Section of Roof of Covered Homestead | 91 |
| 26. | Plan of Stable | 96 |
| 27. | Plan of Double Stable | 96 |
| 28. | Plan of Stable, with Feeding Passage | 96 |
| 29. | Section of Iron Roofs | 124 |
| 30. | Section of Wood Roofs | 124 |
| 31. | Detail of Iron Roof | 126 |
| 32. | Plan of Small Farmhouse | 142 |
| 33. | Chamber Plan of Small Farmhouse | 142 |
| 34. | Elevation of Small Farmhouse | 143 |
| 35. | Section of Small Farmhouse | 143 |
| 36. | Plan of Small Farmhouse | 144 |
| 37. | Chamber Plan of Small Farmhouse | 145 |
| 38. | Elevation of Small Farmhouse | 146 |
| 39. | Section of Small Farmhouse | 147 |
| 40. | Plan of Homestead for Small Farm | 148 |
| 41. | Plan of Upper Storey of Homestead | 149 |
| 42. | Section of Upper Storey of Homestead | 149 |
| 43. | "View" of Small Farm Homestead | 151 |
| 44. | Plan of Pair of Cottages | 158 |
| 45. | Chamber Plan of Pair of Cottages | 158 |
| 46. | Elevation Plan of Pair of Cottages | 159 |
| 47. | Section of Plan of Pair of Cottages | 159 |
| 48. | Plan of a Butter Dairy for a Farm of under 100 acres | 165 |
| 49. | Plan of a Butter Dairy for a Farm of over 100 acres | 166 |
| 50. | Plan of Poultry House and Yards | 172 |
| 51. | Section of Fowl House | 172 |
| 52. | Plan of Poultry Buildings and Yard | 172 |

# MODERN FARM BUILDINGS.

## CHAPTER I.

### INTRODUCTION.

It will not be desirable to commence a treatise on a subject of this kind without making a few brief explanatory remarks upon the object which I hope to attain, and the method by which it is proposed to proceed with the work. The production of a reliable practical guide in the erection of new and readaptation of old farm buildings is the end which is aimed at. The points of construction tending to make the various buildings thoroughly effective for their purpose as independent structures, where they are required to be erected as such, and collectively for forming complete homesteads, will be treated of in detail and illustrated where necessary. The conversion of old buildings into more useful modern purposes will also require attention. At the same time it will be borne in mind that farming systems and practice pursued at homesteads will be of more imperative concern in the future than they have been in the past, owing to the keen competition with foreign products which meets our farmers in every step they take. There must be no waste—and I use the word in its widest sense—either from neglect or ignorance, if farming is to hold its own in this country at the present time. By a due appreciation of this fact, and a careful study of the details of construction and arrangements required, it will be within the power of those engaged in farm building operations to be of material assistance to the farmers themselves in their efforts to secure an economical system of management at their homesteads. These are neither more nor less than food manufactories, and any real improvement therein which will benefit the tenant must of necessity also benefit the landlord, provided of course that it has not been purchased by too costly an outlay. It is not, however, the intention to advocate elaborate and expensive structures; on the contrary, economy must be the order of the day, and be sought for accordingly; but it will be evident that, for the sake of meeting the requirements of home farms, &c., where, owing to the desires of the proprietor, cost of construction is not the main factor, the representation of more complete and expensive buildings must not be omitted. At the same time these will not be without their general use, as they will serve, in a measure, as text plans for instruction and guidance, which will be capable of modified application under different conditions.

As regards the advantages to the owners of estates who, from time to time, have been enabled to equip their farms with sufficient buildings for their requirements, and such as are properly adapted for administering to the most approved methods of farming pursued in their district, there can be no divergence of opinion. Of course no person would presume to affirm that a good set of buildings would be the "making" of a bad or indifferent farm; but it will be safe to say that, as a rule, men of capital, judgment, and enterprise are more easily attracted to farms having good and sufficient homesteads, for without these there is less encouragement to invest largely in stock, which is by many persons still regarded as the most important road to success (on suitable farms of course) in these trying times. The more cattle kept at the homestead the greater amount of manure will be made, which is, as it always has been, one of the chief means of maintaining profitable fertility of the land. In fact, an agent inspecting a farm will generally leave satisfied if he finds plenty of stock, and the land clean; there is then very little fear of the farm or the tenant going the wrong way. On many properties, however, it has been, especially of late years, a matter of impossibility almost for owners to expend what has been desirable in the matter of buildings; but even in these cases a good deal of improvement may be frequently effected at a moderate outlay in many ways, by the adaptation of old barns to more serviceable uses, the use of corrugated iron roofing where suitable, and the judicious use of such materials as can be procured on the estate, which, although perhaps of not very lasting quality, may serve until the advent of better times. It is necessary to be able to make the most and best of small opportunities under these conditions; in fact, we may take it as the opinion of competent persons, that even where there is no lack of funds, and no unwillingness to use them for the improvement of homesteads, it would be a mistake in many instances to expend money in putting up buildings too substantially. We all have a laudable desire to "make a good job," which will be understood to be a very lasting one, as nothing can be so unsatisfactory to an owner of property and his executive officers as to have to be constantly amending recent works. As regards the present farming outlook, everything is unsettled; our best men have, by the reverses of recent years, ceased to rely on their hitherto successful methods;

they have already considerably modified them by other endeavours ; and they are still on the alert with a view to introduce such further departures as may commend themselves for successfully coping with the ever-increasing competition which confronts them. This is hardly a time, therefore, to spend money on elaborate structures, which may almost as soon as they are completed become out of date ; and it must not be forgotten also that the exigencies of the times may necessitate the subdivision of farms into smaller holdings. The need of this is already quite apparent in many districts where the farms are adapted for it, and the principal obstacle is in the expense attending the erection of the additional homesteads, and the reluctance probably to sacrifice the use of a considerable portion of sets of buildings substantially constructed. In this connection I may state that, with a view of meeting the requirements of small holdings, a chapter has now been added on this part of the subject.

I am quite assured that no apology is needed for dwelling at some length upon the agricultural problem, because if farm buildings are to fulfil their purpose as important aids to farming practice, it will always be necessary to obtain an intelligent view of present circumstances, to forecast as much as possible to meet probable future contingencies, and to adapt the means and opportunities to the ends in view accordingly. To become possessed of such information should be the aim, therefore, of all those who are invested with discretionary power in the equipment of farms with the necessary buildings, if success is to be attained. Most of us have seen examples of huge mistakes, and money spent on improvements, so called, which have entailed loss both on owners and occupiers alike—not merely in faulty methods of construction, but chiefly in unsuitability of design and arrangement. These errors, if they were not the result of mere carelessness, must have proceeded from the want of a due and intelligent appreciation of the requirements of the farm, or of the district in which the works were executed. As we proceed it will be shown that farming practice differs so much that buildings which would be really needed in one district or on one farm might be entirely out of place in another. Ideas may be quite correct and up to date in that part of the country where a person has resided long enough to become familiar with it, but they would very likely require considerable modification elsewhere. In commencing practice in a fresh neighbourhood, there are sure to be some customs which, at first sight, or even for a time, would strike us as being wrong in principle; but it is always best to inquire, and to think carefully, when in the course of time it will be frequently found that our new neighbours had more common-sense than we gave them credit for—that experience had guided them in the right direction. It is not always so, otherwise we should never advance and improve upon the ways of our predecessors; but when, after due observation and reflection, a change would seem advisable, it should be carried out with moderation and care. Due regard to the wants and ideas of tenants in the matter of their buildings should always be given, but as a six months' notice may sever their connection with the farm, and as their desires, as may be expected, only represent their immediate wants, irrespective of any other or future considerations which attend upon ownership or otherwise, those in charge of proposed building improvements should always, if possible, be prepared to exercise an independent opinion, based upon an intelligent and common-sense view of all the attending circumstances of the case.

Let me give an illustration to bear upon the foregoing views, and of such a nature as may at any time present itself to any one in practice on a landed estate. A farm, say of 300 acres, with the usual buildings upon it, which are more or less out of repair, and which were needed for and erected to suit the mode of farming practised early in the century, requires some building improvements made upon it. On making a visit, what do we find? That the farming practice has changed to a very material extent, but the buildings have in a great measure remained as they were. By the term usual buildings is meant the all-important barn, of flail-threshing memory, as a nucleus, which is surrounded with one or more large yards, a stable, and a cow-house or open shed for cows. And assume also that, even in these trying times, landlord and tenant both have confidence in their opinion that a moderate outlay of money, one of two or three hundred pounds, may prove remunerative; or it may be that the tenant may say, "I can't go on any longer unless something is done." Well, in order to do justice to the parties interested, the expert in building had need almost to be an expert in farming as well, if he is expected to give an independent and correct opinion as to what is best to be done. It will be quite evident that the barn, as a place for storing corn in the straw, is no longer needed as such, as this can be stacked out of doors and threshed by machinery, or stacked in Dutch barns, which are less costly erections. If it is fairly substantial, it may be converted to some other use. But what are the most pressing needs of the farm? This of course depends upon soil, situation, climate, distance from populous centres, and other considerations. In drawing a distinction broadly as regards the first three of these factors, it may be said that if a line was drawn down the centre of the map of England, on the east you would find the district mainly a corn-growing one, and on the west the dairying and stock-growing industry would be more prominent ; and of course there are marked differences in practice between north and south owing to climatic influences. In the former case, if the farm was not near enough to a large town to be influenced by its requirements for vegetables or green crops or straw, most likely sheep would be kept in considerable numbers ; and if the pasture land was of small extent, preventing the profitable breeding and rearing of stock, one of the main features required at a homestead for such a farm would be warm and comfortable sheds and yards for the economical use of straw by consumption by purchased stock. The barn might be used partly for storing a day's threshing of straw, and the remainder converted into chaff, cake, and meal stores, or perhaps into a store for some of the many implements now in use which require careful housing. If the land was of a stiff nature, and not so well adapted for sheep, it is most likely that there would be a little more pasture, and more manure would be required to be made at the homestead. In this case a range of fatting stalls or boxes might be required, either of which can sometimes be obtained from a barn area, while the upper space can be advantageously utilised as a food-store by placing a floor above the cattle. Then of course there are the customs as regards horses, pigs, or a few cows, to be taken into account, as this is but a very rough outline of the probable points to be considered.

On the other hand, supposing the farm of 300 acres was situated in the western half of the country, or the dairying and stock-raising district, as we have termed it, the building improvements required to the old homestead would very likely be materially different. There would be more grass land and less arable, consequently more stock and less straw, and the soil and climate would be moister; fewer working horses would be kept, but a yard might be required for the use in winter of unbroken horses and colts. Here one of the main objects of the farmer would be to economise in various ways the use of the more limited amount of straw grown; the winter feeding of the cattle of various descriptions would necessitate a considerable proportion of it being eaten, or more possibly "converted" into chaff for mixture with other food substances. Facilities in the building would therefore be required on a liberal scale for chaff-cutting, cake-crushing, meal-grinding, root-cutting or pulping, and storage for the same; and it is under this, or similar conditions, involving the exercise of a large proportion of the farm labour at the homestead itself, that the advantages or disadvantages of a well-arranged set of buildings are made more clearly apparent. Tenants so situated are naturally much more alive to its value than those occupying more purely arable farms; and if due attention is not given by the agent or clerk of works to these matters, they need not be surprised if the tenant himself attempts to solve the problem of a contemplated rearrangement of his steading by enlisting the aid of the village schoolmaster, or some person with a knowledge of drawing, for the production of a plan of his own. Again, as regards straw, by reason of its comparative scarcity in stock-raising districts, it frequently happens that on this class of farms, where they have been within a few miles of a populous town, it has been to the best interests of the tenant to sell a few tons when prices are high, while feeding stuffs were purchased in return for consumption on the farm sometimes at ten shillings a ton less money. The yards for stock should therefore be reduced in size to the least practicable dimensions for the saving of bedding and the better preservation of manure, the waste by washing out and the evaporation being reduced in proportion as it is made deeply and spread over a smaller area. And as proof that there is no standing still even in the matter of farm buildings, our attention has recently been directed to the sanitary condition of cowhouses as a means of checking the spread of tuberculosis.

I have thus shadowed, although of necessity dimly and imperfectly, some of the considerations which must weigh and be properly determined in the minds of those having the control of the building works on farms, if they are to be carried out to the advantage of the owner and his tenant. It does not fall to the lot of every one to gain a practical experience in the work carried on at farm homesteads, which is the best assistance any designer of building improvements can have to hand; but it is quite within their power to foster a habit of inquiry and study of these matters, such as will enable them, with the additional knowledge which may be obtained by a reference to suitable works, to do full justice to any work which may fall to their share to carry out. We must not, however, build solely for present requirements, but as far as possible anticipate, and prepare accordingly, for future changes and wants. This can be done in a great measure, as will be shown, by roofing-in considerable areas in a block to avoid outside walling, and subdividing the interior in light and inexpensive ways with a view to facilitating subsequent alterations. Intelligent practice, with true economy, is the best motto for our purpose; and so far as these principles exist in the works under our direction, they will be the measure of success attained, and of the mark for good which we all hope to leave behind in our handiwork.

## CHAPTER II.

### THE ARRANGEMENT OF HOMESTEADS.

IN designing a complete homestead, either large or small, the main objects to be obtained are to arrange the various buildings so that all kinds of stock will be placed under such conditions as are most favourable to their health and profitable maintenance; to place them as near to their food-stores as possible; to place these food-stores in close relationship to each other in order that preparation and mixing may be carried out with facility; to provide an access to straw for litter, and to give the readiest means for its deposit with the manure in the yards when soiled; and to arrange the whole, having due regard to all points affecting the health of the animals, in as compact a design as possible, and on the smallest amount of ground in order to ensure the least outlay. This is but a brief summary of the general principles which, so far as they extend, should be applied to the erection of homesteads. They will be illustrated by a few examples of complete sets of buildings, and afterwards each building will be treated of by itself with the necessary detail.

As every county or district has its particular customs of farming, and as farms vary so much in their extent and physical aspect, it would clearly be impossible, in a short treatise of this kind, to provide examples of homesteads to suit all sizes and conditions of farms; but to confine the matter to a limit within reach, it is proposed to set forth a type or form of arrangement as a general guide under ordinary conditions and circumstances, and such as will be easily adapted for modification or extension of its component parts to meet the particular requirements of any given case; and similar examples will be given for small holdings in a later chapter.

The first example homestead, Fig. 1, is one designed by the author and exhibited in competition at the Royal Agricultural Society's Kilburn Show, and for which a silver medal was awarded. It was for a farm of 400 acres (100 of which being pasture) and supposed to be highly productive and well farmed, hence the ample accommodation for stock, &c., provided; but for land of ordinary capacity such a design might be equal to 600 acres or even more.

The "best" plan was asked for in this case, and the author has intended it, as a whole, to embrace all the possible needs of a high-class homestead for a farm—chiefly arable, but having a fair proportion of productive pasture —built in the best manner, and with accommodation and fittings suited to the modern requirements of an intelligent and high-class system of farming practice. It is therefore desired that it should be regarded more as a "text" plan, embodying fully every requisite enabling it to fulfil the purpose of illustrating the principles of design and arrangement of the various parts, rather than a plan to be adopted in its entirety at any other, perhaps, than a model home farm for a landowner's use. But although farming wants have here been so amply provided for, it has been done at the least possible cost (having regard to the nature of the workmanship), and the author claims as one of its important—if not its *most* important feature—that the method of arranging the principal parts in one block causes such a saving of material as cannot be obtained in any other way. When the whole homestead is brought into a single block, as will be the case in the subsequent plans which are more adapted for general use, the absolute economy of the system is more evident.

In order to describe and properly explain the features of this design I cannot do better than give the description, which is copied from the report in the Society's Journal, as follows:—

### ARRANGEMENT AND GENERAL CONSTRUCTION.

A large number of the buildings have been arranged in one block, both for economy in building and for the saving of time in attendance upon the stock. The roofs are partly carried on brick pillars 10 ft. 6 in. apart from centre to centre, and the various compartments are divided by dwarf walls 4 ft. 6 in. high, except the stables the wall of which is carried up to the eaves in order to keep the circulation of air quite distinct from that in the yards. The bull-house and the boiling-house are the only other places which will of necessity require the inner walls carried eaves high, except of course if any of the yards are open. This grouping of the parts and dwarf walling materially lessens the cost of building and the time in looking to the stock.

It will be seen that the buildings *fence themselves in*, forming their own roadways very nearly without walling.

*The Yards.*—These can be covered or open, as desired, without any alteration whatever in the general plan. Lean-to shedding could be placed on the south side of the range of food-stores for the two upper yards; and span-roofed shedding for the two lower yards (also open to

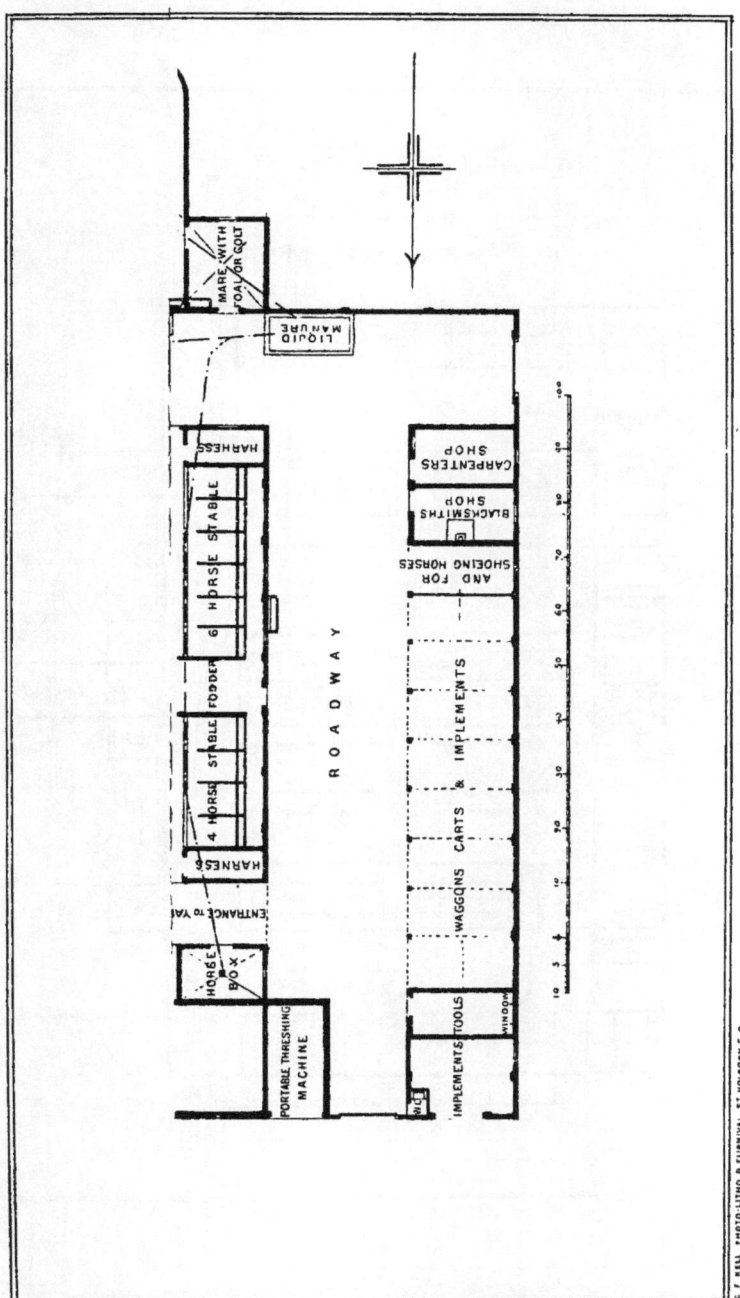

*FIG. 1.*

**PLAN OF**

# FARM HOMESTEAD.

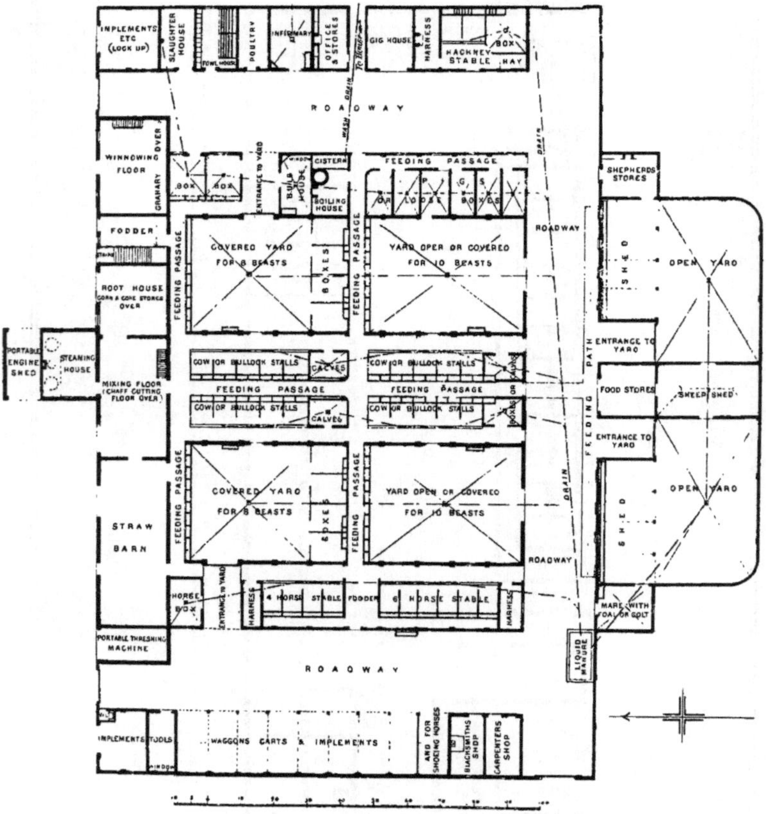


... PHOTO LITHO & FURNIVAL ST HOLBORN E.C.

south), which could also cover in the feeding passage and loose boxes.

*Corrugated Iron a Substitute.*—A saving would be effected by covering any of the four yards and loose boxes with iron instead of half-slating. The iron would be fastened on the purlins, no rafters being required; it can be bought of good quality at about 1s. 9d. per sup. yard, and it may reasonably be expected to last twenty-one years with care, thus being only 1d. per sup. yard per year for a covering to protect both beasts and manure! This of course does not include the timbers, which would not require renewing with the iron.*

*Ventilation.*—Although the main block is grouped to save walling, ventilation is not sacrificed. The eaves of the yards are carried by means of the pillars high enough to give an opening (all along) 12 in. deep above the eaves of the stables and pigsties. Shutters could be put to regulate the amount of air thus admitted if desired. Also, instead of the ordinary louvre boarding in the ridge, an opening 3½ in. deep between each rafter the whole of the length of the roofs is provided by putting a "pitching" piece on to the rafters resting on the upper purlin, and footing the short top rafters on to it.

*Ventilating Shafts under Mangers.*—The ventilating shafts constructed with 12-in. pipes under mangers in feeding passages and having air brick openings every 10 ft. apart, will conduce greatly to the health of the animals standing continually opposite each other in the stalls. The air thus admitted comes into the centre of the buildings covered in, where most wanted.

---

* Since this was written, curved iron roofs have become more general, but they are rather more costly than flat iron on light timbers.

*Light cheaply provided.*—This is done by glazing the space between two rafters on each side between each of the roof principals on each pier. A piece of 2 in. by 1 in. deal nailed on each rafter forms a rebate for the glass, which can then be glazed like a greenhouse. This is cheaper than glass slates, as the glass is only in one thickness, and moreover it gives more light, there being no harbour for dust as is the case between the slates.

*Ventilation of Stables.*—The feeding passages with its windows and ventilating bricks introduce a good supply of light and air in front of the horse. The importance of this arrangement to the horse's health and eyesight cannot be over-estimated. Light is also provided in the roof at back, and same ventilation as for yards.

*Portable Engine Shed.*—The engine can be got in without backing, no small advantage to a farmer. A fixed funnel in roof, with telescopic slide, effects a considerable saving in the height of walling required for engine-sheds.

*Shafting.*—The main shaft for the machinery (which is supposed to be found by the tenant) runs through the roof of the steaming-house, into the most central place for working the various machinery in chaff-cutting floor, corn-room, mixing-floor, and root-house. It is of course worked by the portable engine.

*Water Supply.*—If water is not available in some other form, the best situation for sinking a well would be near the shafting, say in the mixing-room, so that it might be pumped up by steam-power into the 3,000 gallon tank which is provided and forms part of the roof over the steaming-house. A considerable amount of roofing water is conducted into the tank for use as far as it will go. The various troughs in the yards will be supplied from the large tank by gravitation.

*Drainage.*—The ordinary plan of laying drain pipes, with small branches to each cesspool from a main, is departed from; drains of a sufficient size being taken *direct* from cesspool to cesspool. The author has found great convenience in this arrangement for wiring them out when stopped without disturbing the ground and line of pipes.*

*Loose Boxes.*—Box-feeding is provided for only in a limited extent; it will be sufficient, however, for the animals which are not suitable to run with those in the yards. The covered yards are intended to answer the purpose of boxes, and they have the advantage of getting the various manures mixed and well trodden by the beasts.

*Tramway.*—This being expensive, is not provided. It is almost unnecessary, as the feeding passage floors being smooth and made of concrete, food trucks will run very easily upon them, especially if laid, as they might be, with a slight incline from the food-stores downwards. A concrete pathway is continued across the road to the open yard block for use of food truck.

*Pigsties adapted also for Loose Boxes.*—These are divided from the yards by 4 ft. 6 in. dwarf walls between the piers, and the manure made in them can be easily cast over into the yard without any labour of wheeling. The boiling-house is close at hand; but if the food is prepared in the steaming-house, or if they are used as loose boxes for cattle, for which they are equally suitable, there is direct communication by the feeding passages with the food-stores and steaming-house.

*Food-Stores generally.*—It will be seen that the straw

---

* All drains would now require to be carried on the surface of the floors of buildings and discharged outside, as referred to in subsequent chapters on each class of building.

and the various sorts of cattle food, and the means of converting and mixing the same, are placed as close as possible to each other in the two-storey buildings on the north. Any grain or cake stored up in the granary can easily be trucked into the corn and cake room adjoining, ground for the use of the stock, and shot down through the floor to the mixing-room.

*Dunging-out.*—The dunging-out from the whole of the stalls, pigsties, stables, &c., is effected very quickly through the doors provided; or, in the case of the cow-houses and pigsties, it can be done with the cast of a shovel over the dwarf walls, which would spread it also for treading in with the manure made by the beasts in the yards.

*Straw-Barn.*—The straw-barn has communication by doors with the various compartments all along the second storey building, so that a waggon admitted through the doors could unload, under cover, hay for cutting, corn or cake for stock, or corn for granary, which could easily be hand-trucked along the floor to its destination. A load of grain for market could also be loaded up, the corn being trucked from the granary. These advantages would be considerably appreciated by most farmers in wet weather. A good-sized stack of corn could be put in part of the straw-barn at harvest ready to be threshed early for straw. This could be done by the portable threshing-machine being put inside the large doors alongside the stack, and the straw could be stored on the large chaff-cutting floor, or even in one of the covered yards.

*Fowl and Poultry Houses.*—One of these is not fitted up, being left clear for any sort of poultry most desirable to the tenant to keep. The doors of these could be put on the other side of the building, if desired, to open into a proper poultry yard, which could be got at by the mistress from the back of the supposed house without entering the farmery.

*Office and Stores.*—This will be found very useful for business purposes, storing and mixing medicines, &c., and is close to infirmary.

*Slaughter-house.*—This has the advantage of being near to the infirmary for slaughtering any animal found incurable and difficult to move.

*Infirmary.*—This is apart from the other places for stock, and near the supposed position for house so as to be easily got at at night. The drain runs to an isolated tank to prevent infection by connection with the other system of drainage.

*Stables.*—Chaff or pulped food can be brought from the main food-stores for the horses with great facility. The feeding passage arrangement has many advantages, as the fodder can be carried and put in the rack without part of it falling and being wasted amongst the litter, as is often the case. Manger stuff can also be put in the manger from the passage through an open space between the bottom rail of the rack and the top of the manger. It will be seen, however, that the hay and chaff store is accessible from both before and behind the horses, so that it could be used for supplying them in either way. The dunging passage communicates under cover directly with the straw-barn for getting a supply of litter.

*Cart-Shedding.*—The whole of the cart and implement shedding is placed in one block facing the east, the most suitable aspect; these could not be more conveniently placed than they are, being so near the stables. It is also an advantage to have the tool-house in this range, as many tools are required to be at hand to give the carters when they start off to various jobs. The opening in the waggon-shedding nearest to the blacksmith's shop is boarded off to form a place for shoeing horses when required.

*Granary.*—The granary provided is perhaps hardly large enough for a 400-acre arable farm, but it will be found sufficient in conjunction with the winnowing-floor beneath. This winnowing-floor (or part of granary it may be called) *being on the ground floor*, will be found to effect a saving of labour at certain times when corn only requires to be stored for a few days previous to being sent to the purchaser. The stairs leading to the granary also serve for an approach to the corn and cake store as well, from the outside, besides the step ladder from the mixing-floor. Provision is also made for bag-hoisting through doors to both these places.

*Calf Pens.*—These are rather small, but in a usual way there is not supposed to be much rearing on arable farms. The two boxes, however, at the extreme end of the stalls could be used if more room was required.

*Bull-house.*—As the bull-house opens into the entrance to one of the yards, a gate might be put by the roadway, which when shut would form a useful enclosure for serving cows.

*Mixing Floor.*—In speaking of the food-stores, mention was not made of the pair of doors which gave access for a horse and cart on to this floor. This would be found very useful at times to take a load of prepared food direct from the heap with a cart to any part of the farm for the use of sheep, &c. An extra lot of turnips could be stored also on this floor, if desirable at any time, as they would be quite close to the cutters or pulpers.

*Open Yards and Sheep Sheds.*—This block is quite distinct from the main part of the farmery, although in direct communication with the main food-stores. It would be

## Their Construction and Arrangement. 19

found useful for supplementary purposes, such as for young horse stock, for cattle when first taken up from pasture before going to be finished off in the covered yards, or for an exercising ground at suitable times for stock from these covered yards.

The sheep-shed is not fitted up, but is supposed to be furnished by the tenant with such portable fittings as may be required, according to the various uses to which he may put it. At lambing time it would serve for pens for ewes and lambs, the flock having the run of the yards and shelter of the sheds adjoining. It would also do at times for shearing, feet paring and dressing, or as an infirmary for a few cripples or sick; and sometimes perhaps it might be found serviceable for getting a few sheep forward for the show-yard or the butcher. As sheep-shedding is considered rather as an extra, the shed is drawn somewhat small, but it can be easily extended to any length in its present position.

The foregoing explanation of the plan, Fig. 1, will make the aims of the designer tolerably clear. If the main block with its wings on the right and left is divided longitudinally into three parts, it will be found that the centre portion is devoted entirely to cattle and the food-stores; that on the west to horses, carts, and implements; and that on the east, which is supposed to be near the farmhouse, is applied to the more domestic purposes of the farm, that is to say, to pigs, fowls, sick animals, office and stores, nag stable, and coach-house. The "block" or "attached" system has been adhered to as far as possible in giving such extended accommodation, for the sake of concentrating all the work of the homestead (if I may use the expression) and economising building materials. If the southern supplementary block of open yards and shedding was omitted, as it could very well be for many farms without detracting from the completeness of the plan, compactness of design would be secured to a very material extent, so much so that the whole of the work in attending and feeding the stock could be done under cover by the week together if the food-stores were well filled, and with the additional advantage of being able to maintain a neat and orderly appearance without the necessity of cleaning up roadways. The two wings would then be the only detached parts, but as these are placed they fence in the necessary roadways for communication without the erection of walling or fencing. However, on smaller farms, or those of more moderate quality, these parts can be dispensed with altogether, as will be shown in the next illustration, Fig. 2.

As previously remarked with regard to Fig. 1, the design was intended to be a model or "text" plan to illustrate fully an economical system of building arrangement and homestead management on a high-class and fertile farm; but however desirable it may be in these respects, the all-important item of cost is paramount in the vast majority of cases, and a plan giving an example more suited to ordinary everyday requirements on average farms is produced in Fig. 2.

This design, which is for a farm of similar size,—about 400 acres, one-third pasture, but nevertheless it may be properly described as an arable farm,—is intended to reproduce in a modified degree the main features of the former plan. It would be hardly possible that a plan like this, drawn as an example, would be entirely applicable for any particular farm of the size requiring an entirely new homestead; but if any necessary departures to meet a given case could be effected by slight extensions or

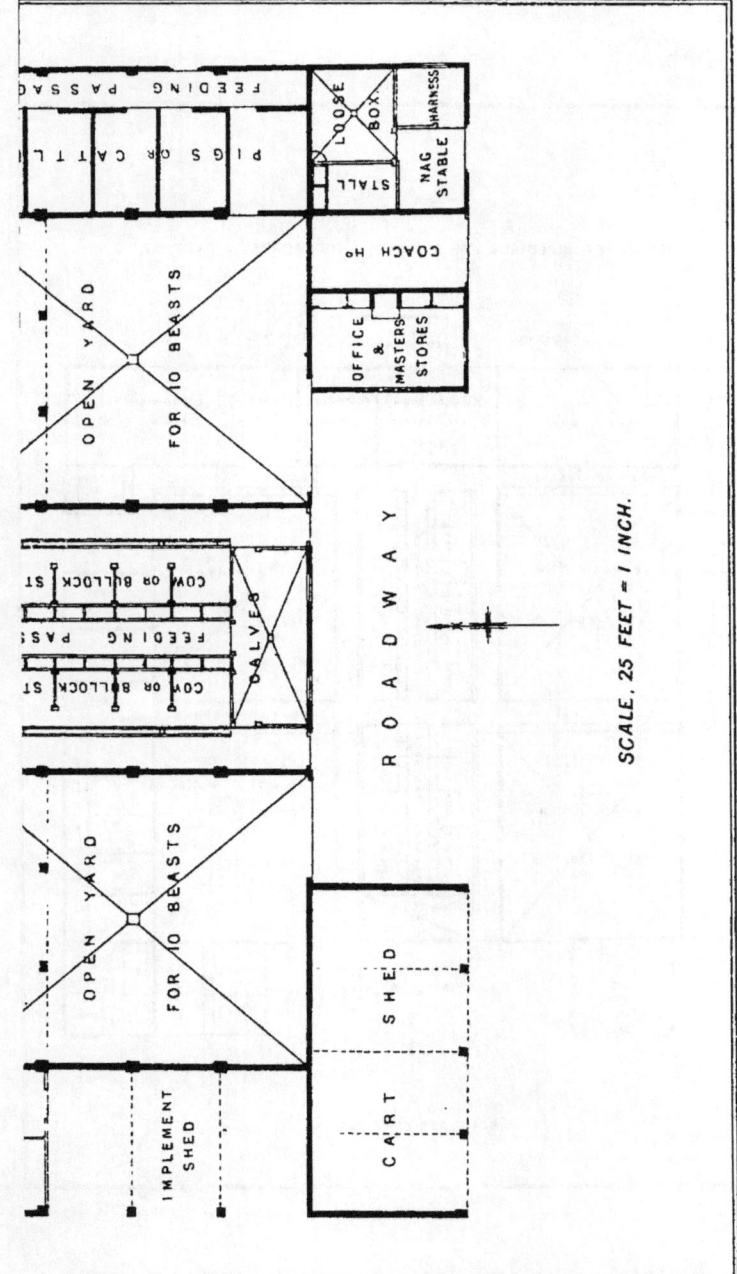

FIG 2.

DESIGN FOR BUILDINGS FOR A FARM OF 400 ACRES, 1/3 PASTURE.

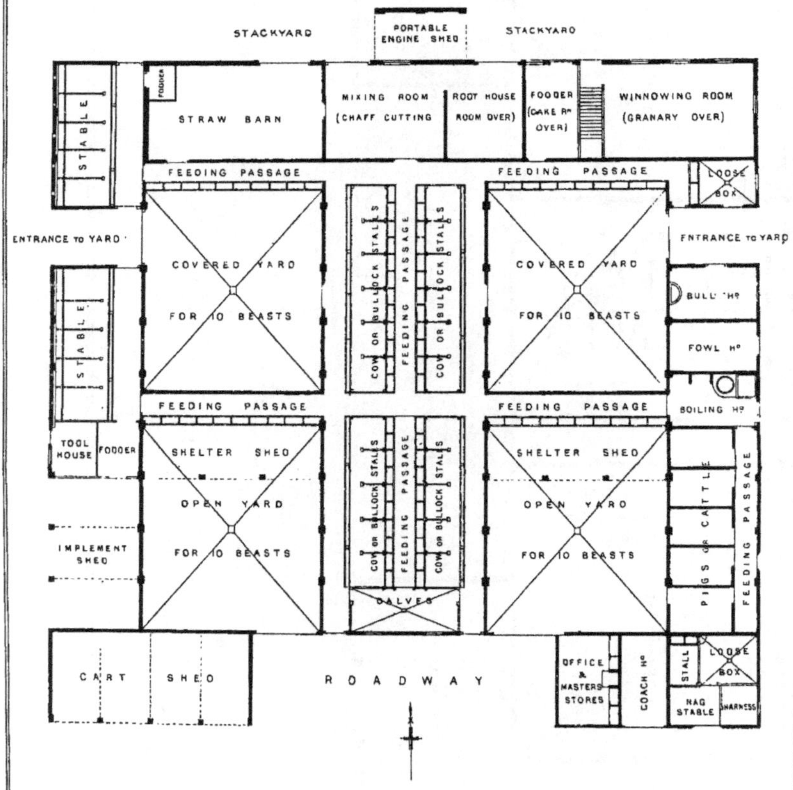


SCALE, 25 FEET = 1 INCH.

## Their Construction and Arrangement. 21

modifications of the various parts, or their fitting up,—and much in this direction can be done,—it will be seen that for compactness and consequent cheapness of construction the design will not admit of much improvement.

The plan was prepared by the writer to illustrate a paper read by him upon the subject of farm homesteads, at a meeting of the members of the Surveyors' Institution, and is reproduced here by permission; and it is almost needless to say, that before presenting it to an Institution which embraces amongst its members many of the most eminent and experienced land agents of the day, it was carefully considered. It embodies all the usual requisites of a well-managed homestead on a farm of the kind to which it applies. On comparing it with the first design, it will be found that the northern two-storey range has been reduced in length to add to the extent of the one-storey building on the western side, by means of which the latter is made to include the shedding as well as the stables, which are returned, as also is the case with the eastern range, round a portion of the south end of the two open yards, leaving room only for the gateways. This is an advantage in protecting the yards against the storms usually prevalent from that direction. There are 44 stalls, either for fatting or dairy cattle, and yards to run 40 more, all easily approached under cover from the food-stores; the horses and carts are close together, as also the fowls, pigs, nag stable, store-room, &c., which are all required to be easy of access from the house, which is intended to be on the same side. Economy of construction as regards arrangement of the buildings has been secured to a full extent, as when they are erected the four cattle-yards are *entirely* fenced in, there being no walling whatever, and the hanging of the doors is all that is required. Moreover, when the two upper yards are covered, as intended, no high walls are required for the central portion occupied by cow-stalls, the roof of which is supported on brick piers and the space between filled up with dwarf walling or a boarded fence. There is, however, one feature which would be better for a slight alteration—the cart-shed at the south side. This faces the south, which is not a good aspect, and it was by an oversight this was not remedied, as intended, by turning two of the openings of the cart-shed to face with the implement-shed, and putting doors to the other two openings for the better protection of the more expensive class of implements; or perhaps it might be better still to reverse the positions of the two side ranges altogether, thus giving the cart and implement shedding an eastern aspect as in Fig. 4, which is the best. In this case the straw-barn and winnowing-room would also exchange positions, and the assumed position of the house also.

The reading of the paper and the inspection of the design led to a lengthy and instructive discussion upon its features, and upon the subject generally, which it will be more useful to refer to when discussing in detail later on the methods of constructing the various compartments forming a homestead. Any further explanation of the various features of the plan will not be needed if reference is made to that accompanying Fig. 1, which gives the author's ideas briefly on the most important points, many of which will here apply, as this plan is a modification of the other.

Before giving attention to smaller arable homesteads, it will be convenient to show how Figs. 1 and 2 can be altered to suit dairy farms of a similar size, as this can be done without materially departing from their main features of construction.

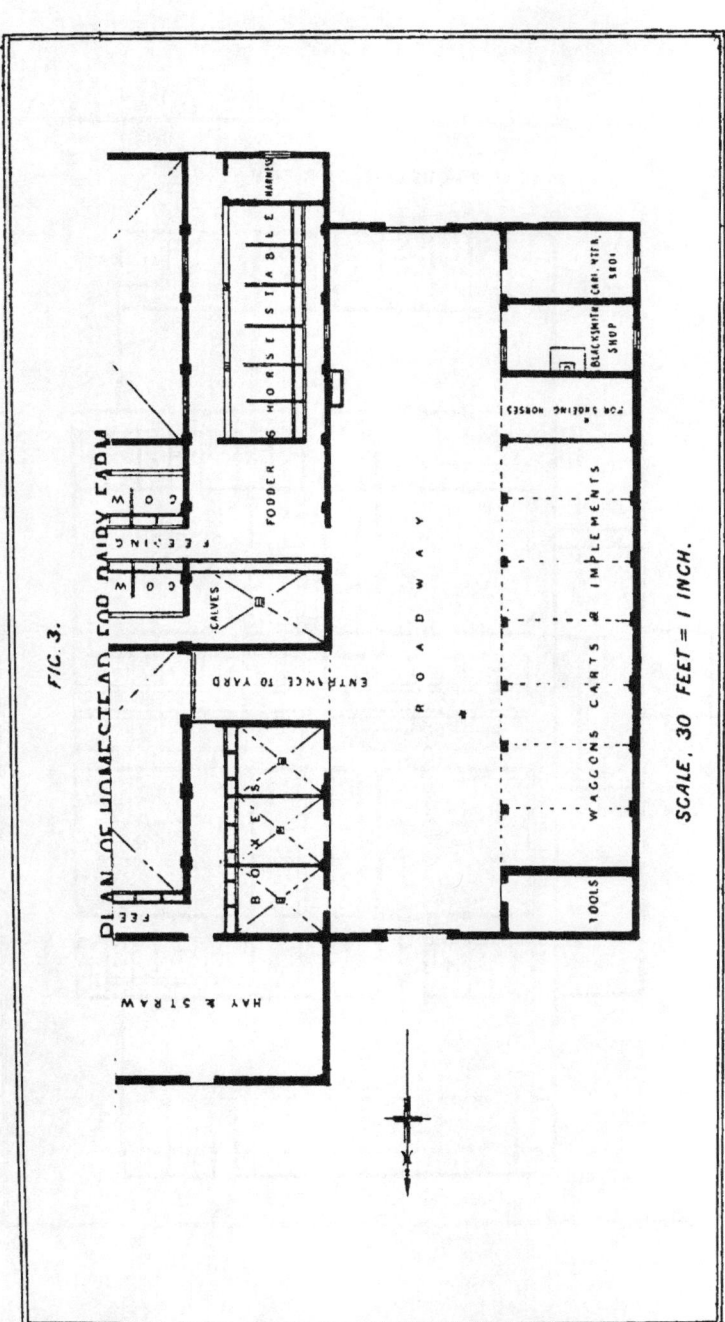

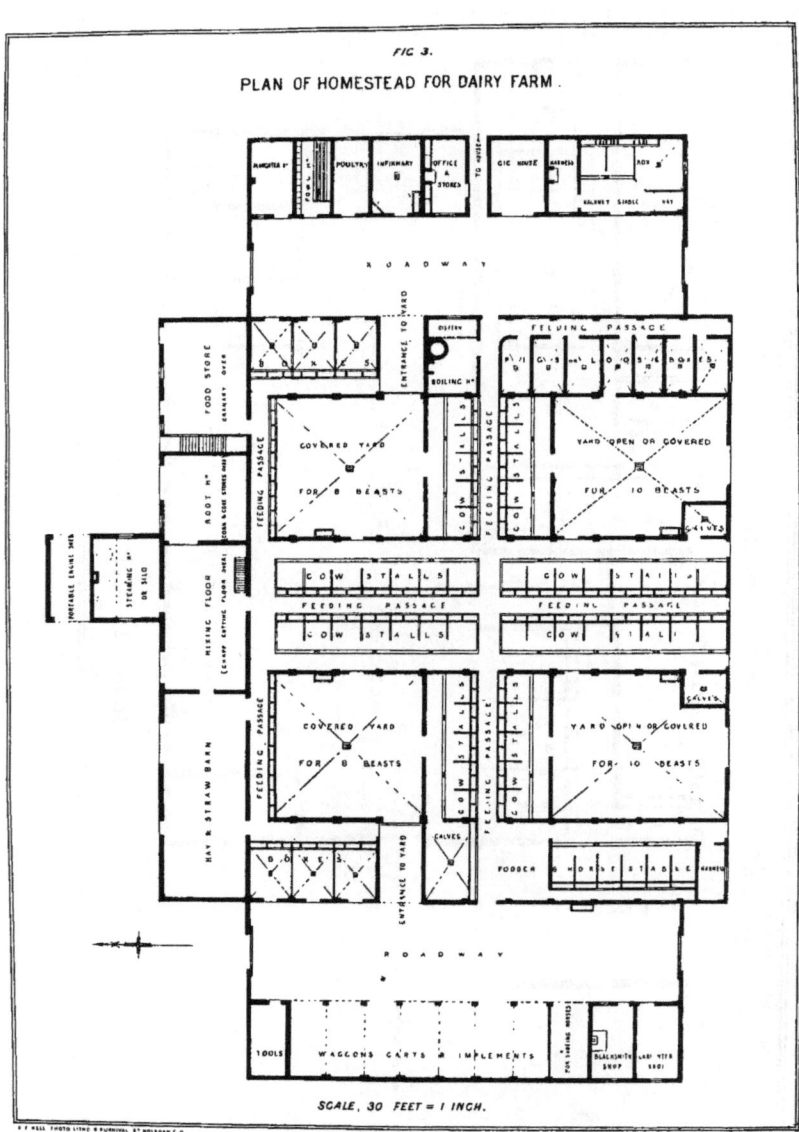

## Their Construction and Arrangement. 23

For this purpose Fig. 3 is given as a modification of Fig. 1, and contains accommodation in the stalls for 100 cows, centrally placed, and easily supplied with food from the mixing-floor and straw from the straw-barn. There are three boxes for calves, and six boxes for bulls, calving cows, &c. On comparing the two designs it will be seen that the two-storey range is reduced in length by taking off the projecting portions. The straw and grain grown would be less, consequently the granary accommodation is limited to an upper chamber only, and the winnowing-floor converted into an extra food-store, as more stock would be kept. The portable threshing-machine would scarcely be needed, and the barn would be available for hay as well as straw. This might be built less expensively if left open on the north side, the principals being supported there on piers on the principle of what is known as a Dutch barn. The main block of building has been extended southwards 11 feet, to add a few more stalls and to keep the yards the same size, after allowing for the insertion of cow-stalls extending east and west, one or both portions of which would be equally adapted for fattening any cows no longer required for dairy purposes, or for bullocks. One more pigsty is also obtained, as pigs would probably be more freely kept. The stable is reduced to accommodate six horses only, and the east and west detached ranges are also curtailed, as less carts and implements would be needed; but the "domestic" portion of these would remain unaltered. As silos are now being used, the steaming-house could be utilised for one, if preferred, or a portion of the space taken up by the straw-barn.

Thus each of the departments is complete in itself, with ample means of communication, and there are no straggling or detached portions difficult of access. The work at such a homestead can therefore be performed with the minimum amount of labour, and the compactness of the design will secure economy in construction. Ventilation, drainage, and light, which are important matters in all dairying buildings, are fully provided on the principle explained in the remarks made in connection with Fig. 1.

Having shown by means of Fig. 3 how Fig. 1 could be altered and adapted for a dairy farm, I will now deal in the same manner with Fig. 2 by means of Fig. 4, which represents a plan of buildings for a dairy farm of 400 acres. This plan occupies exactly the same area as that from which it is adapted, with this exception, that the buildings are not returned round the south end quite so far, thereby leaving the ends of the yards more open and exposed. The central double line of cow or bullock stalls, accommodating 44 beasts, remains unaltered, but two additional cow-houses are added in the side ranges to afford standing room for 16 more, and there are two boxes inserted on the south side, making accommodation in the whole for 62 cows. The two small cow-houses would be as easily supplied with food as the larger one, by means of the feeding passages provided, and although some persons might prefer that they should form part of, or directly adjoin, the main cow-house, it is presumed that their detachment will not be without advantage. It frequently happens that cows which are of no further value for dairy purposes cannot be profitably disposed of except by converting them into beef, and under these circumstances it will be very convenient if such animals can be placed in a house by themselves, such as this plan will admit of. They will be quieter, and consequently be under more favourable conditions for putting on flesh. No extra room has been given for calves, but this could easily and conveniently be

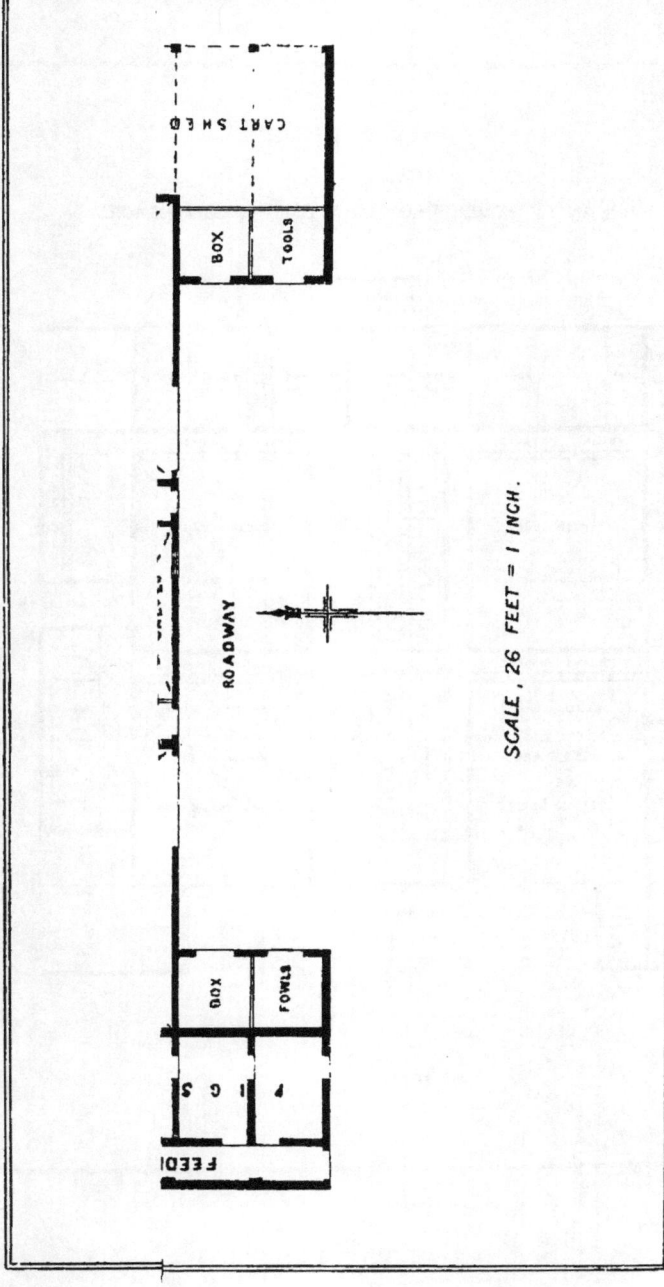

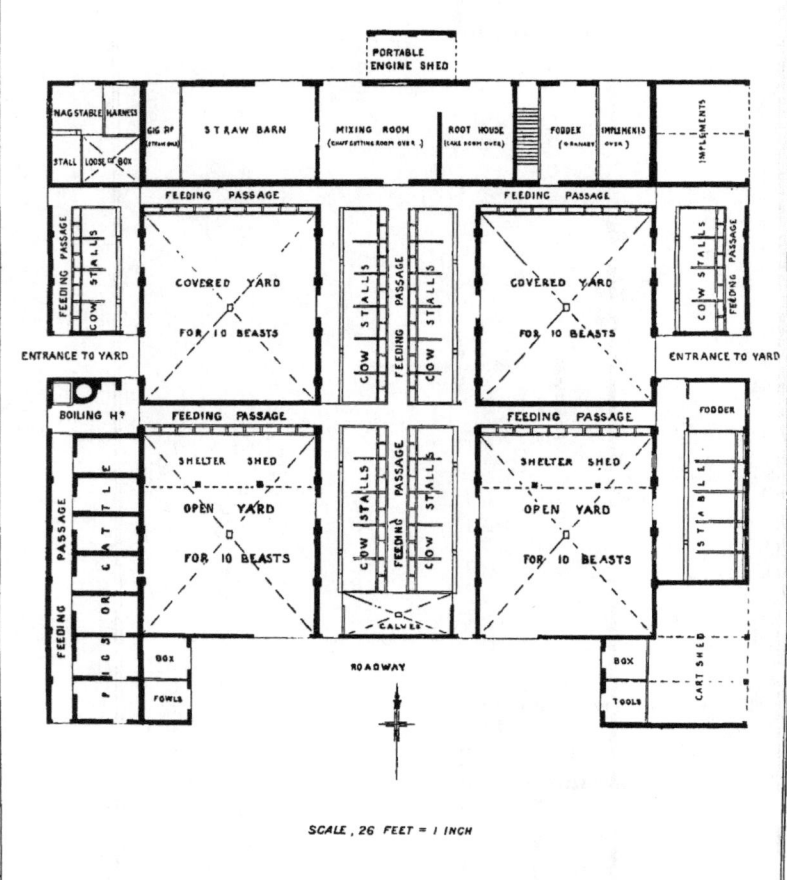

FIG. 4.

PLAN OF HOMESTEAD FOR A DAIRY FARM OF 400 ACRES.

SCALE, 26 FEET = 1 INCH

supplied, if required, by enclosing a small pen or two from the yard area at the back of the stalls; but on many dairy farms the custom is not to rear the young animals but to purchase cows or heifers.

As this design occupies as nearly as possible the same area as that for the arable farm of the same size, it is evident, presuming they are both adapted for their respective requirements, that the cost of equipping farms with suitable buildings would be about the same for dairy as well as for arable purposes; and in practice I have found it to be so. Climate, however, and local customs, have a bearing upon the cost, as in the southern districts, where the winters are comparatively mild and straw cheap, many well-managed dairies of cows are kept in yards with sheds, with but very meagre accommodation in the shape of closed cow-houses; whereas in the northern and midland counties, which are colder, and where straw is more expensive, it is almost always the custom to house the cows at night. The quality of the land also influences the cost of the buildings on a farm in proportion to the amount of stock and crops it will bear. The design under discussion is for land of an *average* quality, and there are of course farms of the size, of a better nature, that would require more accommodation for cows, although we have presumed that, in this case, more than the sixty-two, for which stalls are provided, would be kept; but as some of them would always be dry, these would do very well to take their chance in the yards.

In order to obtain the extra cow-houses the stabling and cart-shedding have been curtailed, there being less arable land; as also the grain stores, which are limited only to a granary on the second floor; and the straw-barn is reduced by taking a gig-house out of it. On the other hand, two extra pigsties are given, as pigs are usually more extensively kept where much butter-making goes on, as a profitable means of disposing of the skim milk.

It will also be seen that in this plan the stabling and cart-shedding have been put on the east side of the homestead, instead of the west as in Fig. 2, as in dealing with that design we stated that it would be an improvement to obtain a drier aspect for the storage of carts and implements.

As regards the southern ends of the yards being, as previously remarked, less closed in by buildings, a few words on this point may not be out of place. It has been customary in the erection of homesteads to leave these quite open and free for the action of sun and air, and to many persons the plan would appear to be badly arranged because they are not so. This was the case with some members of the Surveyors' Institution, who criticised the similar arrangement in the design, Fig. 2, at one of their meetings at which it was produced for discussion; but from experience I think otherwise. The rays of the sun would enter the yard over the roof of the buildings and the entrance gate quite sufficiently to give its occupants the benefit of the "sun-bath" which is material to the growth and health of young animals, therefore this advantage is not lost; and on the other hand, the shelter which the buildings afford is in some cases invaluable in protecting cattle from the severe storms of wind and rain coming from the south and west. Many yards with this aspect are almost useless in bad weather, the animals being in utter discomfort whether in the sheds or out, as they (the sheds) are open to the same aspect, and profitable consumption of food under such conditions is almost out of the question. In some situations the necessary shelter may be otherwise obtained from local surroundings; but where this is not the case, it is certainly advisable, if possible, to procure it by means of a high fence, or by arranging some portion of the buildings in the position of those shown on the plan, or otherwise placing them so as to attain the desired effect.

The foregoing remarks may also apply, in a measure, with regard to the shelter shed of the lower yards abutting upon, and closing up, the ends of the covered yards, which they do to a great extent, although not entirely, as the upper part of the gable is left clear. This, and similar points of detail, will be discussed later on, when the construction of each building is separately dealt with (I am now only treating of the general arrangement of homesteads by means of the accompanying illustrations); but from observation, I am of opinion that many covered yards have not fully answered the favourable expectations of their owners, simply because of the ill effects of the powerful cross draughts induced by openings too large in the ends and at the sides. Nothing can be worse than a draught, and animals would be better in open yards than to be subjected to it. A properly constructed covered yard ought to be similar, as regards its temperature and the other conditions of its atmosphere, to a well-ventilated cow-house.

It is not proposed to multiply the example homesteads indefinitely, as it is not necessary for the purpose, which is merely to supply a means of illustrating the main principles which it is necessary to observe in producing serviceable designs. Fig. 5, which is a plan of a smaller set of buildings, to accommodate 200 to 250 acres of land, chiefly arable, is therefore the last design of the kind which will be introduced. The principal features of arrangement in the former plans are again reproduced. The range of two-storey buildings is similarly placed on the north side, but is on a reduced scale. There would be room for taking in several tons of hay on the chaff-cutting floor for convenience in cutting up, and the roots and the mixing-floor are close at hand. A single cow-house, for twenty cattle only, together with two yards, is considered all that is necessary for the animals likely to be supported on a farm of the size, although, as previously remarked, this depends much upon the quality of the land. They could be fed with facility from the feeding passages provided, and the dung from the stalls would be easily deposited in the yard adjoining. There are two shelter sheds to each yard, but although this is the case it must not be considered altogether an extravagant arrangement. One of them by itself would not be of sufficient capacity for the size of the yard, and as the design seemed to lend itself to the present arrangement, which enables some advantages to be gained at a very slight extra cost, it has been availed of to illustrate them. Where one shed only is provided to a yard, the animals must either be fed in the open, where the food is exposed to rain, or the mangers be placed in the shed where, as the animals will be continually standing in it to feed, they will foul, to a greater extent than is desirable, the litter which would otherwise afford them a comfortable bed. This is felt more particularly of course where straw is scarce and valuable. Some farmers prefer one method, and some the other, and it is often a matter of discussion as to which involves the lesser evil. To meet the difficulty, two small sheds for each yard have been provided, instead of one larger one; those abutting upon the north range are in lean-to form, just covering an animal feeding at the manger, and might be constructed economically of corrugated iron; the others, one facing east, and the other west, are only 20 feet long, but of good depth. As the yards are so com-

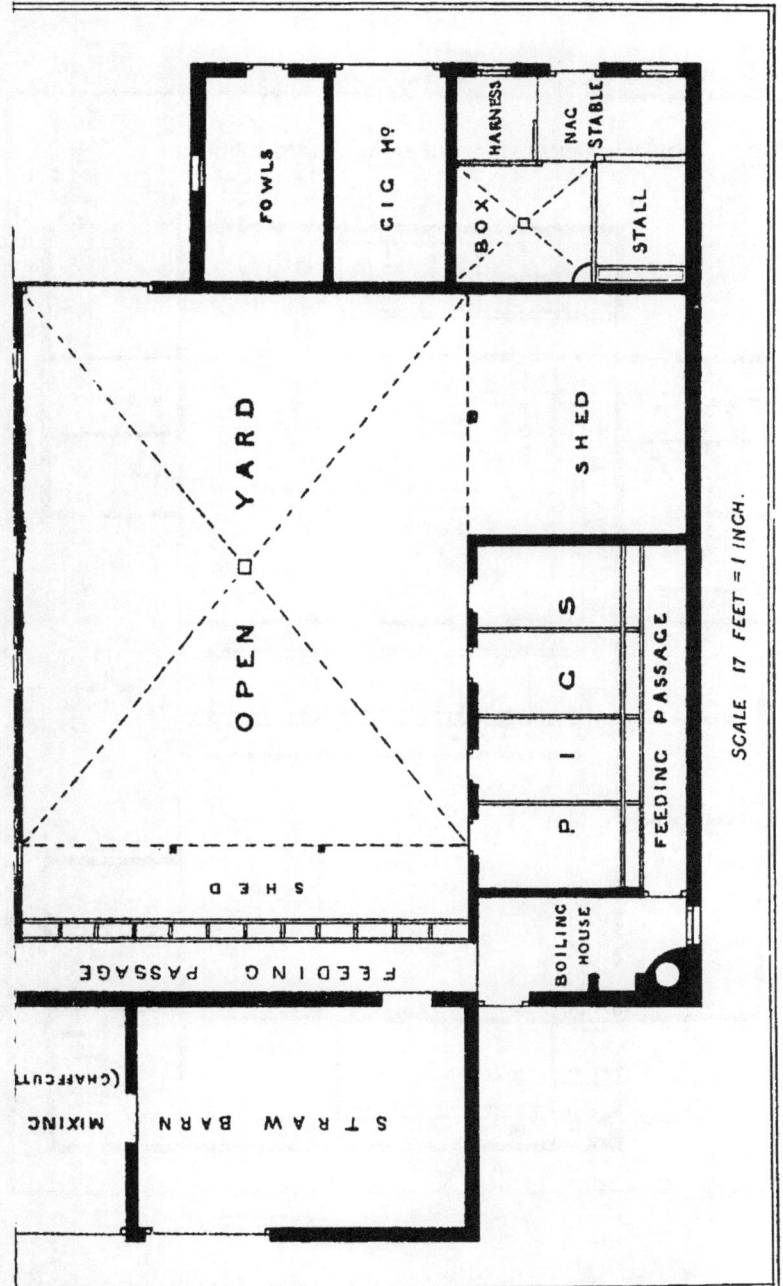

FIG. 5.

PLAN OF HOMESTEAD FOR ARABLE FARM. 200 TO 250 ACRES.

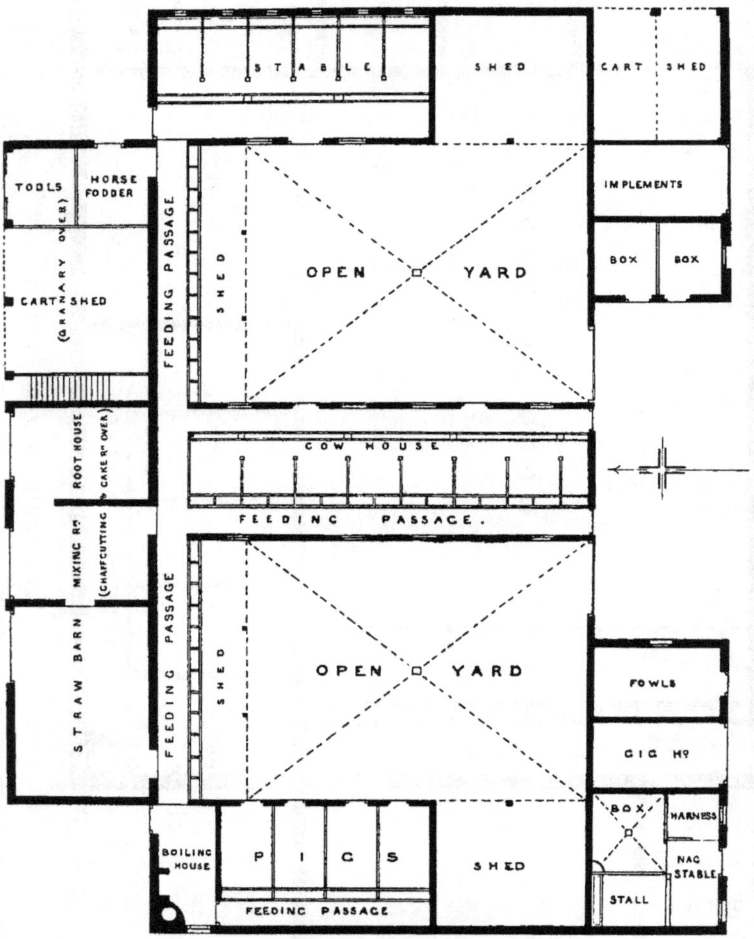

SCALE 17 FEET = 1 INCH

pletely sheltered by the buildings around them, the latter would, under any conditions, afford complete protection to animals, although they would hardly accommodate the ten or eleven in number which the yards would each of them hold; but the other sheds over the mangers would serve for the remainder, and would, from their south aspect, be otherwise very serviceable, although the bedding in them would generally be more or less poached and wet unless litter was very plentiful.

The design still preserves the principle of the larger ones, in placing those parts which have a natural working affinity in close proximity to each other, the eastern side being devoted to horses, carts, and implements; and those sheds at the north, under the granary, are equally to hand from the stable. The pigsties, fowls, and nag stable are all on the west side, where it is supposed the house would be. Many persons prefer the pigsties to be entirely under cover, as shown in the plan, where they abut upon a yard in which the pigs can be exercised when necessary, as when constructed in this form they are convertible and can be used for calves or yearlings, or for moderate-sized cows; but if the ordinary arrangement of sties and yards should be preferred, they could be well placed, with a south aspect, on the site occupied by the nag stable and fowl-house, these buildings then to occupy the space so vacated. It will hardly be necessary to give a separate design for a small dairy farm, *i.e.*, from 200 to 250 acres, as the present plan would be so easily convertible. The number of stalls could be doubled by widening the present cow-house, which would be the chief alteration required; or, if this gave more space than was necessary, a small cow-house could conveniently take the place of the pigsties, which could be placed where the nag stable and fowl-house are, these in their turn being removed to the vacant angle adjoining the straw-barn.

I have now brought to a close this part of the subject. It is not very often—indeed it is quite seldom—that those who are engaged in professional work of the kind on estates are called upon to design a complete homestead ; but if they do not possess a fair idea of the accommodation and conveniences which it should embody in its entirety, they cannot expect to meet with a due measure of success in the numerous works of restoration, improvement, and addition to existing homesteads which have often to engage their attention. A perusal of the foregoing remarks, and of the text plans accompanying them, will therefore, it is hoped, not be unprofitable to those seeking information on the subject, even though they may never be called upon to design a complete homestead.

## CHAPTER III.

### THE REMODELLING OF OLD HOMESTEADS.

IN order that the remarks to be made upon the alteration of old homesteads, and the converting of barns to more modern uses, shall have proper effect, they are illustrated by two plans of work of the kind which have been executed. In the first chapter, reference at some length was made to the problem to be solved when such matters were undertaken. It is certainly a difficult one, as on the one hand the question of cost, which may be limited to a defined amount, has to be considered; while on the other hand the tenant's ideas and wants have to be encountered, which frequently tend to the opposite direction, and are by no means so limited or clearly defined; and further, as there are a large proportion of farms which are more or less suited to alternative systems of farming, each requiring somewhat different buildings according to the ideas of the tenant for the time being (who may give six months' notice to quit after the new works are completed), it follows that, if justice to the landlord is to be done, the style of farming to which an occupation is most profitably adapted must receive due and independent consideration, and the additions and alterations adapted as far as possible thereto. A view of future probabilities and contingencies should also be taken, as this often causes the wants of the moment to be modified, and the works directed to more permanently serviceable channels.

There can be no doubt that errors have been almost as frequent, on some properties, in improving existing, as building new homesteads, from a want of knowledge and forethought; and a decided attempt should always be made to look at all contemplated improvements from every possible point of view. Mistakes arise from the following, amongst other causes. Take, as an instance, the case of a farm the land of which is of very moderate quality, and on which it has been the custom for many years to breed and rear or buy in cattle, to be sold again in store condition. On such a farm the accommodation for cattle would be chiefly in the nature of yards and open sheds. The tenant may leave, not being very successful, perhaps, and his successor comes upon the scene. He intends to farm differently, and persuades the landlord, or his representatives, to put up a lot of stalls and boxes, because he believes that the only means to make the farm pay will be to fatten his cattle, instead of doing business in store beasts. The time comes, however, perhaps in a year or two, when it is found that the land is not good enough to allow a profitable fattening of the stock, and the new buildings then become of little or no use at all. Or, to take another instance, the tenant of a farm, which has usually maintained with fair success a certain quantity of sheep, becomes discouraged by the ill effects of a few wet seasons upon his flock, and determines to give up, or nearly so, the keeping of sheep, and to try his hand at keeping more stock. Extra buildings are asked for, and obtained, this being done almost on the spur of the moment; but afterwards, on the return of more favourable conditions, the extra cattle are abandoned for a return of the flock, and the extra buildings thus become no longer serviceable. Again, there are always farmers to be met with whose ideas run on specialities such as a favourite breed of cattle, sheep, or pigs. Some of these are far-seeing and safe men, to whom it may be of advantage to give the extra buildings they require; but others, as soon almost as they have succeeded in obtaining additions for some kind of stock or other, thereby rendering one class of accommodation abnormally large, and out of proportion to the usual requirements of farms of the kind, may part with their favourites, and the additions to the homestead made for them are of no further value.

In the hope that the preceding observations may put some of the less experienced readers on their guard, we will refer to the illustrations. It must, however, be admitted that many, perhaps the majority of tenants, have views on the subject which are perfectly sound, and worthy of full consideration.

Fig. 6 is the first of the two plans referred to as illustrating the alteration of old homesteads, and the work was carried out for the seventh Duke of Marlborough on an Oxfordshire mixed farm. The existing or old buildings which were allowed to remain are shown by the "cross-hatched" outlines (that is, those filled in with sloping lines), and the new buildings are drawn black. It would hardly be possible, without confusion, to show on the plan the buildings which were pulled down—they were very meagre, and consisted merely of a worn-out wooden cow-house and cattle-shed stretching along the south-west side of the enclosure, which then formed a very large, uneven, and badly exposed yard, over which the cattle could roam at will, and the place was well adapted for wasting, instead of preserving manure.

C

On examining the old buildings, it was found that the stable, barn, and cart-shed were substantially built with stone and slate, and it was decided to let them remain; the chief part of the barn, however, was altered and adapted for food and grain stores. After removing the worn-out and inadequate buildings referred to, there remained no accommodation whatever for cows or other cattle, the farm being adapted to carry at least thirty in number, and it became necessary, therefore, to erect such buildings as would accommodate them. The north-west side of the enclosure was bounded by a good wall, and this was taken advantage of and slightly raised to support the roof of a line of open shedding to face the south-east, and serve as a shelter for three yards, which were enclosed by new walls and other new buildings, and divided with strong post and rail fences into moderate-sized enclosures, to allow of the manure accumulating a considerable thickness. A space for a roadway was thus formed between the yards and the other buildings—that is, the stable and the barn which was made into food-stores, &c. A gate was inserted opposite the stable door to conveniently dispose of the soiled litter from the horses; a range of pigsties was built in one of the yards nearest the existing pigs' food-house, with outlets opening into the yard to obtain a run out for the pigs; and the pigs were to be fed, through "shoots" in the wall, from the roadway, as being the easiest method. A house containing ten cow or bullock stalls and a loose box was also added, to complete the block of yards and buildings for stock; and it will be observed that narrow feeding-sheds were placed over the mangers of two of the yards, on the side nearest the barn, the food being inserted from the roadway and cow-house passage through openings in the wall. The roof of these sheds was a lean-to of 9-feet

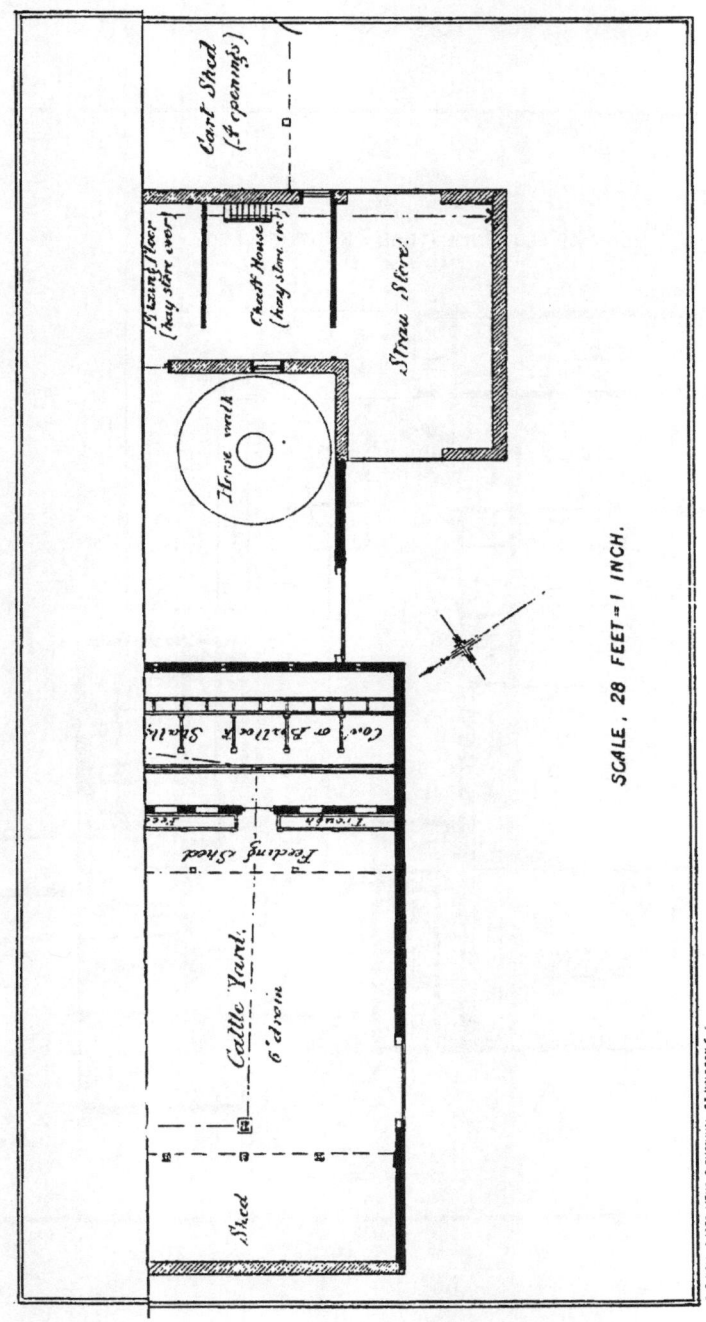

FIG. 6.
PLAN OF OLD HOMESTEAD RE-MODELLED.
Nº 1.

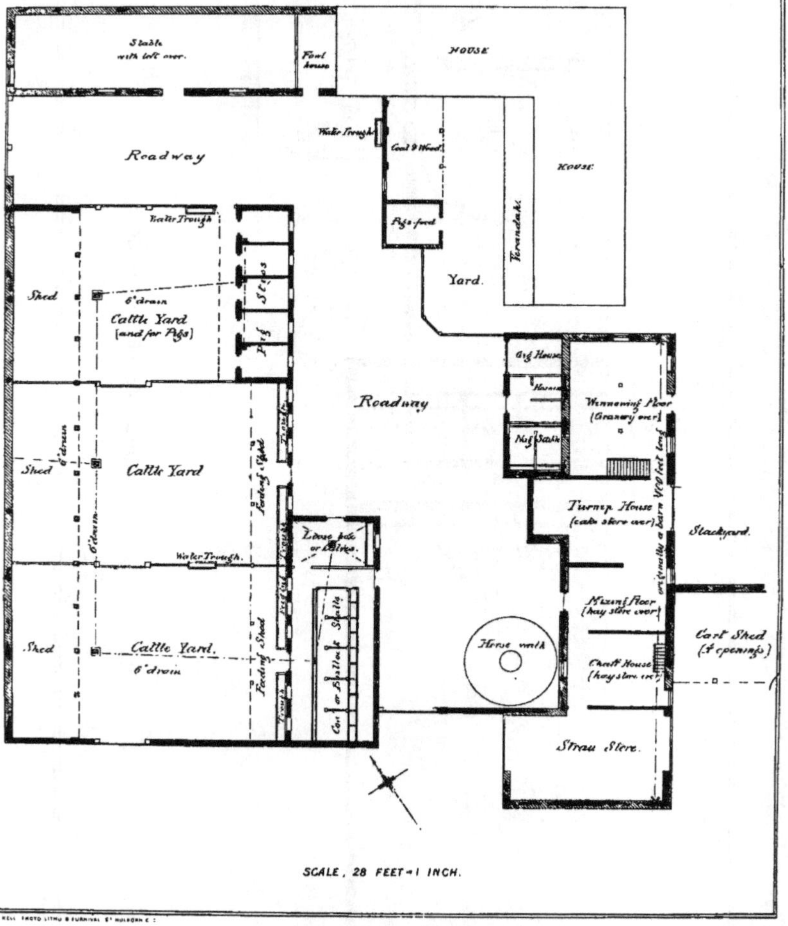

SCALE, 28 FEET = 1 INCH.

lengths of corrugated iron, and consequently of the cheapest description.

Perhaps the most noteworthy feature in the alteration to this homestead is the readaptation of the barn, which was 100 feet in length, and, as previously stated, very substantially constructed. As it lent itself most admirably to supply the range of food-stores necessary for the cattle, and also proper granary accommodation, by a moderate outlay in subdividing the interior by partitions and flooring, the opportunity of obtaining these was availed of in the manner shown by the plan. On the ground floor is a straw-store 32 ft. by 20 ft. (this occupying also the space upwards to the roof), a chaff-house, a mixing-floor, a turnip-house, and a winnowing-floor. The flooring above these provided a hay-store and a cake-store, also a granary approached by stairs from the winnowing-floor for storing all grain for consumption. From the mixing-floor a door opened on to the roadway, which had merely to be crossed for feeding the whole of the cattle in the yards and stalls. A further advantage was taken of the barn walls for building economically a lean-to nag stable and gig-house, in a convenient position near the house. The only remaining portion of new building not yet referred to is a coal and wood house, inserted between the pigs' food-store and the house, thus closing in that side of the house-yard, and breaking the force of the wind on the house, the site of which was much exposed, being on a bleak hillside.

The alterations and additions to this homestead furnished the farm with a convenient set of buildings at a moderate outlay, and properly adapted to its requirements. The cart-shed may seem to be somewhat out of place, being so far from the stable, but as it is on the route to and from the work on the farm, this would not in reality be the case.

The main point studied throughout was to place the cattle-yards and cow-house in a position of easy access from the barn, as it was seen at a glance that this was too good to pull down, and was more adapted for a food-store than for any other purpose.

The second plan of a homestead remodelled is shown at Fig. 7, and is a representation of works executed on the same estate as the previous design, the same distinction also being followed in the drawing between the old and the new parts.

On examining the homestead as it originally stood, it was found that the only portions sufficiently good to remain were the cart-shed, two barns (now converted, one into a granary of two storeys, and the other into a straw and chaff house with a chaff-cutting floor over the chaff-house), and the nag stable. The buildings condemned were a stable and some open shedding for cattle, both of which, even if they had been in repair, were quite unsuitable as regards convenience of access, and in other respects, for their purpose. The yards extended from the boundary wall on the west to the stackyard, and the area they covered was so large that the manure was scattered all over the place and its goodness dissipated by the elements, and the roadway for communication between the parts ran through them. On the whole, a more unsatisfactory condition of matters could scarcely be met with.

The improvement of the homestead presented considerable difficulty, as the approach to the stackyard was either through the yards, or, by a tortuous course, past the front of the house. This is not now apparent, as a continuation of the cart-shed, which embraced a fowl-house also, extended up to the end of the house, but this was removed to form the entrance to the roadway. The boundary wall on the

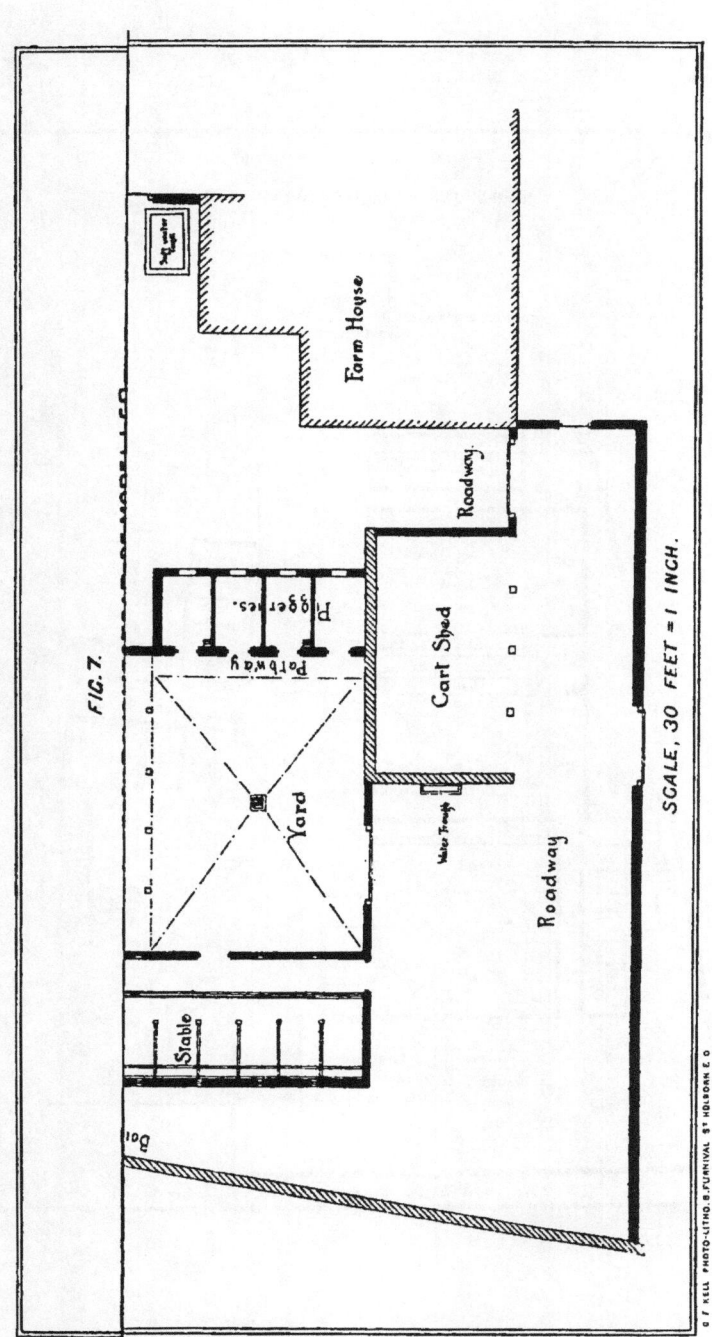

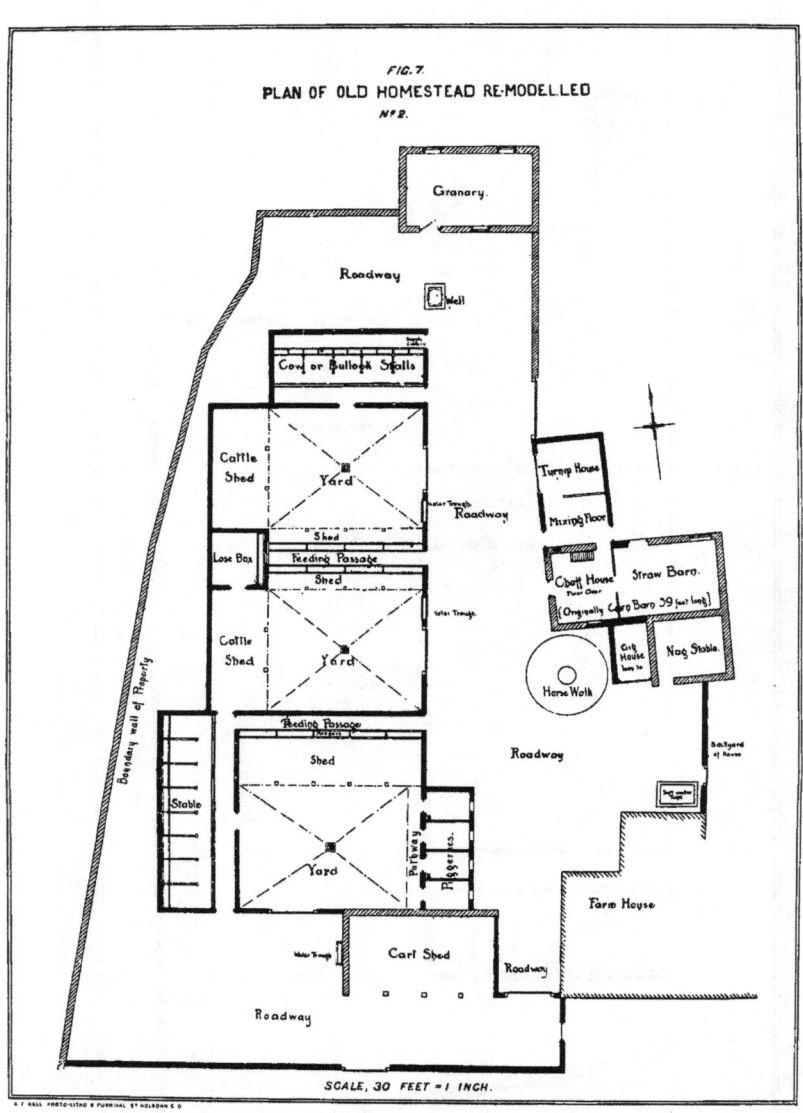

west, at the back of the sheds, happened to be the limit of the owner's property in this direction, therefore the area for improving the homestead was restricted to its existing dimensions, unless the stackyard had been entrenched upon, which for many reasons would have been objectionable and costly. It was somewhat curious to find in this instance, as well as in the case of the previous homestead, that the barns were the most substantially constructed and best preserved of any of the buildings, and that here also, by fitting up the interior, they furnished nearly all the food and grain stores required. In the present plan, a mixing-floor and turnip-house only were added, to communicate with the chaff-house and complete this department.

In arranging the new buildings—those for the cattle and horses—it was first determined to place the stable in its present position near the cart-shed, and to reserve the space nearer the food-stores for stock. Three fold-yards were necessary, and by arranging the new shedding in its present position they were fenced in on three sides, leaving only those adjoining the roadway to be walled up. The cattle were thus thoroughly well protected from storms from all quarters, as the stackyard, house, and adjacent buildings formed a considerable screen on the exposed side. Food is easily supplied to all the yards, and to the cow-house (which is also new), by means of the feeding passages and the feeding-shed running between the two yards ; but it was inevitable, unless other disadvantages were incurred by a totally different arrangement, that the roadway should intervene between these and the food-stores. Of course, in designing a wholly new homestead this could, and ought to have been, avoided ; but the labour of feeding the animals is reduced to a minimum, in the stockman having to cross a sound road with a barrow or hand-truck, as compared with walking across a yard of manure with the burden on his shoulders.

The pigsties are constructed on the same plan as in Fig. 6, with outlets into the yard adjoining the stable, and food would be supplied from the roadway through small doors in the wall. A corner was found by the nag stable in which to build a lean-to gig-house; and a good loose box was formed at the end of the feeding-shed, which completed the homestead in a satisfactory manner. It will be seen that the stable can be entered from the roadway, as well as from the fold-yard, which is a convenience when it is occupied by cattle; and it can also be approached from the direction of the stackyard, chaff-house, and back of the farmhouse, by means of the feeding passage of the cattle-shed, which saves the time both of master and man in travelling round to the entrance from the roadway, which otherwise they would have to do.

In the process of altering and improving homesteads, it will be found that the barn is that part of the buildings which more often lends itself to a useful alteration. Two examples in the foregoing plans have been given where they have afforded accommodation as food-stores, but of course they are often as well adapted for other purposes. Farmers when they complain that they have not sufficient buildings on their farms, do not realise the fact, which is often the case, that if the barn space was properly applied to modern requirements there would be little to complain of. When a suggestion of interference with this ancient institution is made, it is not always approved of; but you can thatch corn and straw, or cover it cheaply in Dutch barns in the stackyard, whereas you cannot thatch your cattle and implements. Landlords originally supplied barns for the purpose of threshing corn in by hand, and there is no reason at the present time why they should be provided, or allowed to stand as such, if required for other purposes, except so far as one, or a portion of one, may be required to house a few loads of straw in a handy position for chaff-cutting or for litter. This will spare everyday visits to a straw-stack in the stackyard, which is a wasteful practice, as it is impossible, when continually taking small supplies, to leave a stack weather-proof.

The lower part of barns can often be made into excellent implement-houses or cart-sheds, but usually they are more suited to the former, as unless there are plenty of openings for getting articles of everyday use in and out—such as carts—inconvenience will arise, and there are many implements which may be stored, one behind the other, which, although very necessary, are but seldom used. Moreover, it weakens an old building too much sometimes to pierce the walls for extra openings for getting carts and waggons in and out.

Barns may also often be fitted up for stock of all kinds, either as stables, cow-houses, or loose boxes; and frequently when the floor is utilised thus, or as cart-shedding, they will also admit of being converted into two-storey buildings, as in Fig. 6, by which means their storage capacity is considerably augmented. Of course the stability of the walls will determine the advisability of subjecting the building to the strain of a floor to form the upper storey. Where it is possible to put in a floor, the joists will often be found useful to steady any stall-posts below, or posts forming boxes; and the work of digging holes and the insertion of posts will be reduced, as a comparatively light piece of scantling may be used for posts, which only requires to be inserted in the floor a few inches when it can be fastened to a beam or joist above. These certainly are small considerations, but they all "weigh" when trying to solve the problem of how to make a good job with a limited sum of money to expend.

Many barns have been condemned to be taken down because their walls were not considered strong enough to support the new roof which might have become necessary, but in such cases there would have been the alternative of using corrugated iron on the very few light timbers which are required for fixing it upon.

In concluding the remarks upon this part of the subject, I should recommend that, before setting out any new buildings at a homestead where a corn-barn exists, an examination should be made with a view to utilising it for one of the purposes which have been referred to, if, all circumstances considered, it would be desirable to do so. I am well aware, however, that tenants like to retain barns for the storage of grain in the straw to save the expense of thatching; but where landlords are ready to meet their wishes in this respect, it will frequently be found that it is better to put up what is known as a "Dutch barn," in a position which is most convenient, as they are inexpensive when constructed of corrugated iron. The site chosen may be in the stackyard, whereas the barn may be near the stock, and may be made serviceable for chaff or food.

## CHAPTER IV.

#### FOOD DEPARTMENT.

STRAW, CHAFF, ROOT, MIXING, AND GRAIN STORES.

IT is only in recent years that farmers have realised the importance of preparing and mixing the various products of their farms, instead of giving them to their live stock whole, or, as it may be termed, manufactured; and consequently, in old or unimproved homesteads, no such means will be found for carrying on the work in the way which is usually provided at the present time. There can be no doubt that numbers of farmers have been compelled by sheer necessity—more particularly in grazing districts—to resort to this practice, owing to the increased demand for meat and the low price of corn. Heavy soils, difficult to cultivate and uncertain in their results, have been given over to grass; less straw has been grown; and it has been necessary to economise its use by cutting it up, instead of allowing animals to pick it over, and tread a great proportion under foot.

Apart from the foregoing reasons, there is another important advantage to be gained when a farmer is in a position to prepare and mix the food for his cattle. By so doing he is comparatively independent of bad seasons, those excessively dry or unusually wet, when straw, hay, and roots have been either a very short or very inferior crop—to wit, the tropical summers of 1868 and 1893, and the deluge of 1879—seasons when stock farmers were put to a severe test to winter their stock. When supplies run short, or are inferior, it is possible by chaffing and pulping, and by adding feeding stuffs, to make raw material palatable, which would otherwise be rejected by animals, and to make that which is good go much further. If farmers are not now in a position to avail of such advantages, the necessity for which most of them have been taught by dearly bought experience, they are often forced to market some of their stock when prices are bad, or otherwise to keep them on such food as barely maintains life.

It is not, however, in the years only of short supplies of straw and hay when advantage is gained by facilities for food preparation. In these hard times it has not always been wise to bind tenants to consume the whole of this class of produce on their farms, as was usual when no expenditure was incurred in purchasing cake and other feeding stuffs; therefore sales of straw and hay have been permitted on many estates, which, when not abused, have been of material service in counteracting the effects of low grain values upon the tenants. By disposing of the straw and hay at the homestead without waste,—that is, by cutting and pulping,—they have been enabled, in years of good produce, to sell a portion of these crops to meet their cake and manure bills. Of itself, straw does not possess a manurial value of more than 12s. per ton, according to good authorities; and when it fetches say £4 per ton, it cannot be a bad investment to sell that which can be spared at this price and to buy good linseed cake at £9 per ton, which yields, as compared with straw, a manurial value of about £3 per ton after its use as a food for cattle.

All these matters are more or less well known and appreciated by farmers; but the reasons for referring to

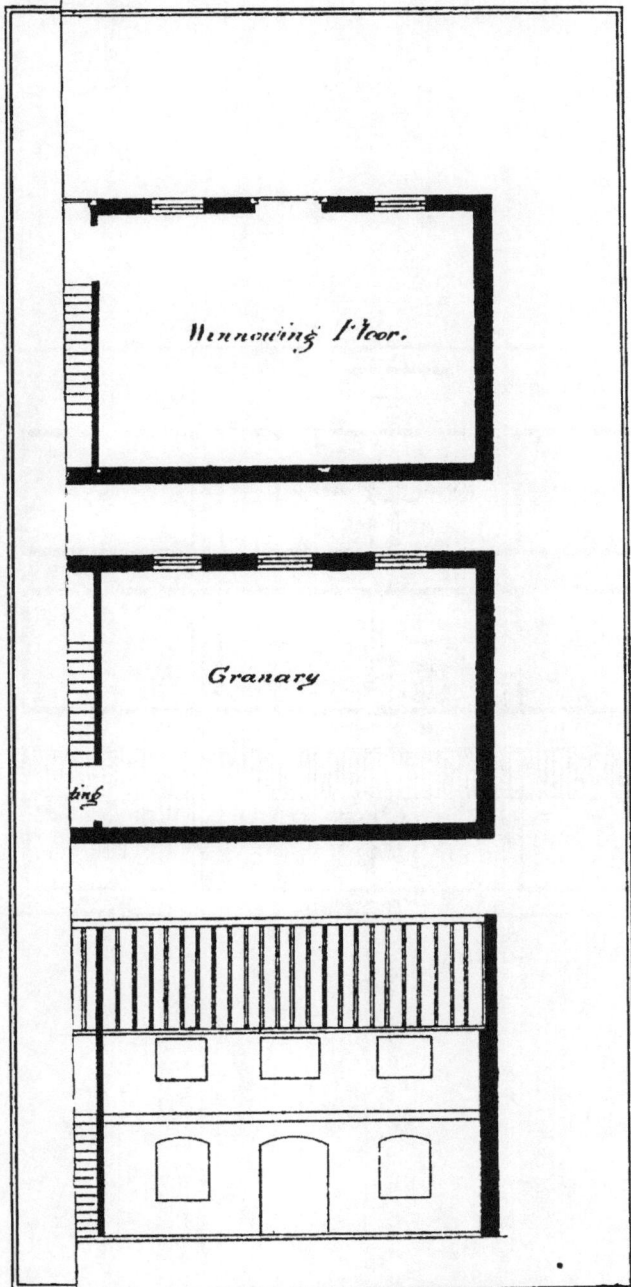

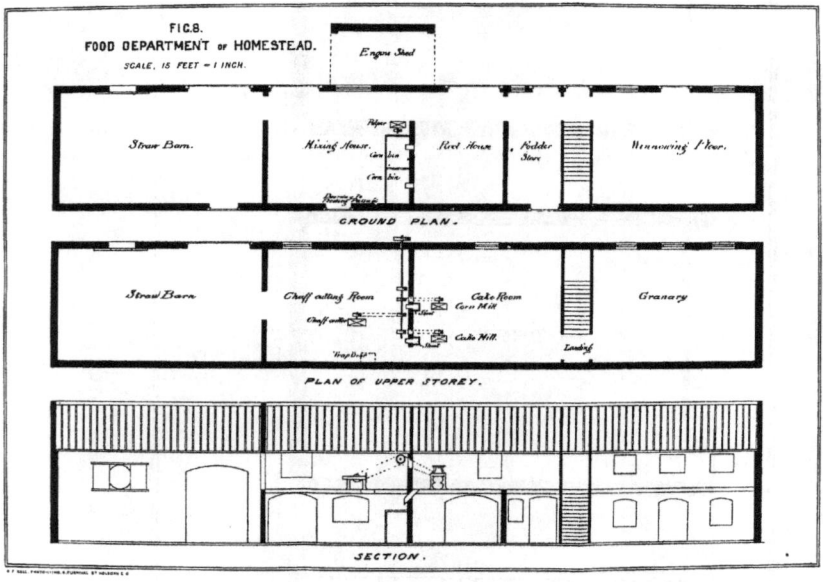

them here is with a view of assisting those whose business it is to conduct farm building operations, and who are not conversant with farming economy, to an intelligent appreciation of farmers' needs in the matter of food-stores. It is not wise, of course, to go in advance of the ideas of a tenant, and incur expense where it would not be attended with corresponding advantage. This might probably be the case if buildings for the purpose in view were recommended for farmers in corn and sheep districts, where much straw is grown and few cattle are kept; but such buildings are invaluable in the hands of intelligent men occupying grazing or dairy farms.

Fig. 8 gives the ground plan, plan of upper storey, and a longitudinal section of a set of buildings forming food and grain stores for a farm of about 400 acres, and this will be all that is needed to illustrate the details of construction and arrangement about to be referred to. The size and nature of any given farm will of course determine the form and extent of such accommodation, although it may not necessitate a departure from the principles which we shall advocate as likely to lead to good results.

First as regards the situation of the food-stores. As they are generally composed of two-storey buildings, and are consequently higher than those provided for stock, it will be advisable, for obvious reasons, if possible to place them on the north side of the homestead, and also that they should adjoin the stackyard, as is supposed to be the case in the various homesteads illustrated. If the yards and cow-houses can be made to abut upon them without the intervention of a roadway, the stores will then be placed between the hay and straw stacks and the cattle which are to consume them, thus minimising labour as much as possible, and avoiding the expense of making and keeping clean a roadway to approach the various stores. The doorways to these will be in the stackyard, where a proper roadway is required for approach to the stacks, and it can thus serve for both purposes.

The straw-barn in Fig. 8 is 34 ft. long and 20 ft. wide in the clear. It is ample for its purpose, which is mainly to take in the straw from a day's threshing so as to be easy of access either for chaff-cutting or for litter. Advantage, no doubt, would be taken of the barn for filling it with such corn, at harvest-time, as would be threshed out early before cattle were brought into the yards for the winter, and the barn be required in connection with feeding them. A pair of large doors are provided, although they are not absolutely necessary for a straw-barn, but they will be useful to take in a loaded waggon, or a load of hay or cake, the contents of which could be easily transferred to the chaff-cutting floor, and, as regards the latter, trucked on the cake-store —these operations going on in rainy weather, when otherwise they might be stopped. It is necessary that the doors should be twelve feet high, and that a small door or bull's-eye opening be placed somewhere under the eaves, to provide the means of filling the other part of the barn if that portion by the doorway is utilised. Openings or doorways are placed as a matter of course for passing hay or straw into the chaff-cutting room and the mixing-floor below, and another door leads outwards to the stock department for carrying out litter. It will not be necessary to say much about the paving of the floor. The whole should be covered with some material providing a fairly smooth surface; that portion upon which the waggons would travel must of necessity be strong, either hard paving bricks, or bricks on edge, or, better still, cement concrete. Bricks laid flat, or thinner concrete, or even a well-rammed earthen floor, will be sufficient for the remainder; but wood floors are decidedly objectionable, as in the long run, if not in the first instance, they are more costly, and they harbour vermin.

The chaff-house, it will be seen, occupies the floor above the mixing-house. There are several reasons why it is desirable to place it in the upper storey; it is convenient for unloading upon, and for lowering the chaff when cut in the quantity needed upon the mixing-floor, exactly in the place where it is required, this being done by means of a trap-door. The position of the chaff-cutter is shown, which is driven from the shaft (also indicated on the plan) that serves for the crushing and grinding mills, and the pulper, this shaft being driven by a portable engine standing in the shed adjoining. One window only is shown, but this would not be sufficient of itself, and light should be given from the roof, the best of all places, by means of glass tiles or otherwise. The same should be done in the case of the barn, and in both cases without stint, as the importance of light where any class of machinery is in use cannot be over-estimated. Floor joists of extra strength are needed for attaching the chaff-cutter to, on account of the vibration of the machinery; and the floor boards should be grooved and tongued, or bonded with hoop iron, otherwise a shrinking of the boards may cause dust and dirt to fall through.

The cake-room, or store, is also placed on the upper floor, for the same reasons as the chaff-room. It is shown as a separate compartment, and is intended also as a store for any purchased corn or other feeding stuff; but unless the feeding of cattle is practised to a large extent it might fairly be dispensed with, and the granary be utilised for the purpose, as there is a winnowing-floor below. At any rate in smaller homesteads an endeavour should be made to combine the two compartments in one, in which case a small portion might be parted off for the cake. Taking the illustration as an example, however, of convenient arrangement, it will be seen that in the rear of the two mills (the positions of which are shown) two "spouts" are inserted to deliver from the floor the cake and meal into bins in the mixing-room below, to be at hand with the chaff and roots. These bins can be provided with lock-up covers if necessary, and the labour of carrying or wheeling the stuff is thus avoided. If there is no room on the mixing-floor for the bins, the spouts might remain for delivery, and the bins be placed in the cake-room itself, in which case the mills should be raised on a platform so as to deliver the material direct into the bins.

The root-house is placed next the mixing-room, just inside which the pulper is placed. It is better to be there than in the root-house, but the division wall at that point should be low enough to allow of the pulper being fed over it. The requirements of a good root-house are very simple. There should be a pair of doors eight feet wide, high enough to admit a loaded cart; a strong and fairly smooth floor; and the back and side walls should be free from door or other openings, so that the roots may be piled high against them. Yet how frequently we see them made much less serviceable by the non-observance of one or more of these conditions.

A fodder store is provided in the present plan, and it is intended for the best hay, which is given "long" to the stock, or for similar uses; but in the case of smaller farms this compartment might very well be dispensed with.

As regards the mixing-house, very little requires to be said, as its use, after the remarks which have been made upon the other compartments, will be tolerably apparent to the merest novice. It is certainly a place of modern introduction, but it plays an important part in the economy of the homestead. It not only serves for mixing up, in considerable quantities, the chaff, pulped roots, and cake and meal, before serving it out to the cattle, but it provides a floor on which the same can lie for a day or more until the moisture introduced by the roots, or by some other means, induces a slight fermentation. This practice is frequently resorted to by farmers, as the process of fermentation renders inferior hay more palatable, and softens the woody fibre of very ripe straw. Like the root-house, it should have doors to admit a cart to load up chaff, &c., going to the sheep-fold, or to outlying cattle; and the floor should be smoothly paved, or concreted, to ensure an easy passage for a shovel upon it. Its position, above all, should be central, as is the case in the illustration, where all the food constituents, after being cut, pulped, or ground, fall into position on its floor, and merely require the cast of a shovel to heap them together.

The engine-house has a lean-to roof, and it is assumed that a portable engine is to be used to drive the machinery, such as will also thresh the corn. Being open at both ends, the engine can easily be drawn in, instead of being backed in, which is a troublesome process. The floor should have a groove in it for the wheels to travel along, to ensure the engine taking a correct position for connecting the driving belt with the shafting. The roof does not require to be high enough to admit the funnel; it is better to have a fixed funnel or chimney in the roof, with a telescopic slide attached for lowering upon the flange of the engine funnel when the upper portion is turned down. If a fixed engine is used in lieu of a portable one, the position of the engine-shed might be the same, or it might take the place of the fodder store. Oil-engines are becoming popular, and one of 3 horse-power which costs £85 I have recently seen in use. The owner says it will work forty hours without going near it, and it burns ¾ pint of oil per horse-power per hour.

There now remains only one other portion of the food-stores to be mentioned, that provided for corn. In the design a winnowing-floor is shown below, and a granary above; but if one compartment only was given, it would, for a 400-acre farm, require to be somewhat larger than the granary, as it should be borne in mind that there is no barn-floor available for storing and dressing the grain. The advantage of having winnowing done on the ground floor is in saving the trouble of hoisting it up to a higher level; and such grain only as is not going at once to market, or that which is required for home consumption, is intended to go into the granary above, where it can be easily trucked across the landing to be crushed or ground by the mills in the cake-room. On smaller farms, or those having only a moderate proportion of arable, one compartment should suffice, particularly as many threshing-machines are now capable of turning out samples of corn which are fit to go direct to market without winnowing. Under any circumstances, the design should provide for the easy transfer of corn in store to the crushing and grinding mills.

## CHAPTER V.

### COW-HOUSES.

UNDER this heading it is proposed to deal with the accommodation for housing dairy cattle and calves. On purely dairy farms the cow-house is naturally the most important building required for stock, therefore every detail connected with it should receive a full share of attention; and as regards arable and mixed farms, there are few of them that do not require more or less limited house-room for dairy cattle.

If an architect is instructed that stalls are required for a specific number of cows, he will so far be clear on this point; but it will often happen to those in charge of landed estates—that is, the estate officials, to whom my remarks are more particularly addressed—that they will have to decide, in conjunction with the tenant perhaps, how many stalls it is necessary to provide for the cow stock on the farm under treatment. To arrive at a fair estimate, the general remarks previously made as to the locality, climate, and custom influencing the character of homesteads, should apply in this department. In some parts of the southern counties it is not an uncommon practice to keep cows in an open shed and yard, the cows being tied up in the shed; but this wasteful custom is becoming apparent to the tenants, and, as one step towards a more economical treatment, a limited number of stalls in which to tie up the newly calved animals are now generally provided, leaving the others to the yards. In the Midlands, and more northward, owing to a difference of climate, and probably also to a truer perception of the art of milk manufacture, if we may use the term, stalls are generally required for housing all the cows on the farm, or nearly so.

I shall refer more particularly later on to the beneficial effect of moderate warmth upon the animal frame, but for the present it will be sufficient to say that a given amount of food, eaten with comfort by animals which are properly protected from the elements in winter, must yield more meat or milk than if consumed under opposite conditions, in which case a portion would be required to replace the heat abstracted from the body by its contact with rain and a cold atmosphere.

It must now be borne in mind that recent legislation has empowered local sanitary authorities to deal with all cow-houses in their district, as their bye-laws will show. These have been more or less stringent according to locality where any sale of milk goes on, and to the ordinary agricultural mind this savours of carrying matters too far; but at all events, in the case of alterations and new erections, it will be better to keep in view the possibility of a visit from a zealous sanitary inspector, who might require alterations to bring the building up to the standard of sanitary efficiency required by the local authority. It is, to say the least, unpleasant to all concerned to have to alter recent work, and a visit of the kind would be almost sure to take place if an outbreak of scarlet fever or diphtheria occurred in the neighbourhood.

But by far the most important factor for consideration in cow-house construction has arisen since it has been proved that cows are frequently affected with tuberculosis, and

## Their Construction and Arrangement.         51

that the milk from them is capable of transmitting the disease to the human system. Under the Dairies and Milk-shops Orders of 1885 and 1886, regulations have been made from time to time by local authorities respecting the sanitary condition of cow-houses, sometimes to be lost sight of, but occasionally administered more or less strictly; but as a result of the now prevailing opinion that the responsible authorities should take further action, the Local Government Board has drafted some well-considered model regulations for the guidance of local authorities. As it is probable that these may be extensively adopted, with perhaps slight modifications, they have been added in the Appendix at the end of this book, and their perusal will afford some valuable information upon the requirements of an up-to-date cow house. The Board's recommendations will, however, be duly taken note of as the various points of construction to which they refer are reached, such as proper space, light, ventilation, paving, and cleanliness.

The following extracts from a leaflet issued by the Royal Agricultural Society in 1899 will also be found instructive:—

Tuberculosis, known also as consumption, wasting, and pining, is a contagious disease, and is spread by the introduction of the tubercle bacilli into the bodies of healthy animals along with the food or drink, and in other ways. Diseased cattle eject bacilli in coughing; also in the discharge from the mouth and nose, and in the manure.

All animals which are affected with diarrhœa, cough, or wasting should be removed from contact with other animals.

Overcrowding, imperfect ventilation, dirt, and darkness favour the spreading of the disease.

An open-air life is the most desirable for milch cows, and under such conditions tuberculosis shows very little tendency to spread.

The cleansing and disinfection of cow-sheds is essential, and the free use of water is a most important part of the process. Sweeping and dry brushing, and the raising of dust, should be avoided.

That the decided effort which is now being made to arrest the spreading of consumption and other forms of tuberculosis in man will gradually lead to the enforcement of strict precautions against the sale of milk from tuberculous cows cannot be doubted; and it is of the utmost importance that dairymen should realise the necessity of doing everything in their power to eradicate tuberculosis from their herds.

Fig. 9 is the ground plan of a single cow-house. As regards the width, 3 ft. 6 in. is allowed for a feeding passage, 2 ft. for a manger, 8 ft. 6 in. for the length of the "standing"

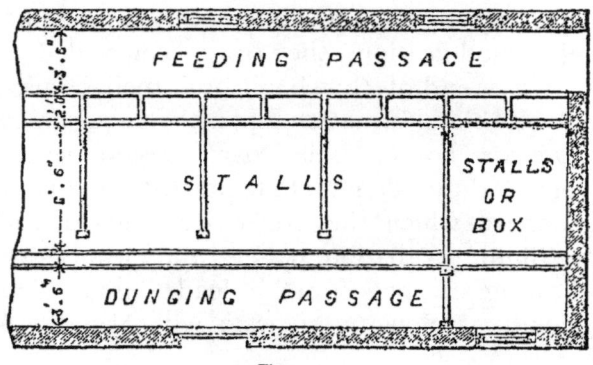

Fig. 9.

and drain behind, and 3 ft. 6 in. for the dunging passage, making 17 ft. 6 in. in all. The standing space is parted by stall divisions 7 ft. apart from centre to centre, each division taking in two cows. These are the recognised dimensions of the majority of cow-houses in dairy districts where large cows are kept, and give every satisfaction, but sometimes of course the feeding passage is omitted. A less space given in any respect is not sufficient, unless in regard to the 8 ft. 6 in. length of standing room and drain, which may be curtailed a little in the case of small cows; more space, however, is not needed for any class of cows.

Naturally different ideas prevail, some persons preferring a separate division for every cow, but in that case 4 ft. or 4 ft. 6 in. of width is required for each animal, and consequently economy of space is sacrificed unnecessarily.

But the question will arise as to what is a sufficient cubical area for a cow in a cow-house. The 17 ft 6 in. by 3 ft. 6 in. of superficial area is 61 ft. 3 in. superficial per cow, and with a height of 11 ft. to half-way up the roof, 673 cubic feet is provided per cow. This is quite sufficient for farmers' cows which are usually turned out daily, assuming of course that other points of construction are favourable to the maintenance of a pure atmosphere; and a perusal of the model regulations before referred to, in the Appendix, will show that no special area for this class of cows is recommended. It will be seen, however, that for other cows which are not habitually turned out, the minimum area of 800 cubic feet is considered necessary, and the reason is obvious when we know that frequently in close urban surroundings cows are continuously tied up and fed largely on grains and other purchased foods. The foregoing dimensions therefore, recommended as suitable for ordinary farm cow-houses must be increased, in one or more ways, to give 800 ft., but it will be quite evident that however liberal the area may be for either class of cow-house, sufficiently pure air will not exist if the floor is defective and retains moisture and dirt, or if the ventilation is inadequate.

Figs. 10 and 11 are plans of double cow-houses. On farms where a large amount of this class of accommodation is needed, it can be supplied at less cost in one of these forms than that given in the preceding figure.

In the first of these designs there is a central feeding passage, while in the latter the dunging passage is in the centre; in each case there is the saving of the width of the one or the other, two rows of stalls being served by one passage. As no more walling is required (except of course at the ends of the building, if it is detached), for the double than for the single form of cow-house, it is clear that a considerable saving is effected of bricks and mortar, and

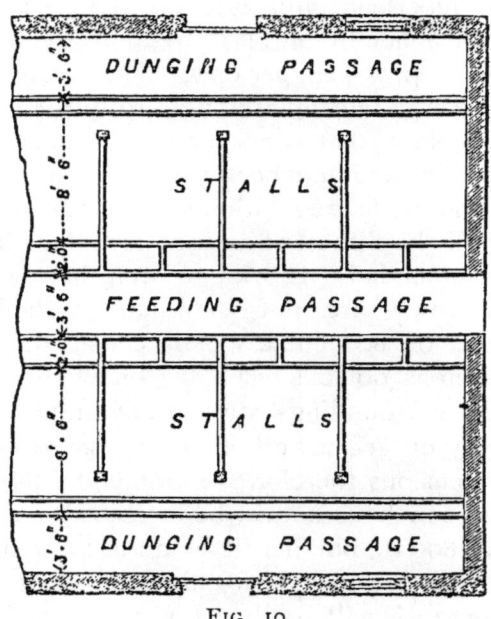

FIG. 10.

of roofing material and labour also. It is sometimes said, however, that any economy thus effected would be counterbalanced by the extra cost of constructing a roof of so wide a span as 32 ft. between the bearings, this being the width of the double building, but this is an erroneous idea.

One example of the construction of roof timbers suited for the span of a 32 ft. cow-house is given at Fig. 12, which

## Their Construction and Arrangement. 55

is economical and effective, and it looked extremely well where it was erected.  The principals are 4 in. thick, tapered from 9 in. below, to 7 in. at the upper extremities. There is a kingpost of the same thickness, the trussing of the roof being effected by two ties of 9 in. by 1½ in. deal, notched in on each side of the principals about half-way up,

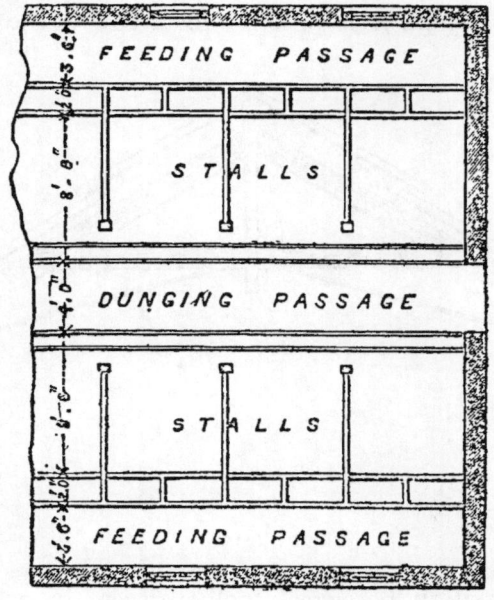

Fig. 11.

a bolt securing them to the foot of the kingpost, which also fastens two light iron rods at the same point, these being run through the ends of the principals and fastened there with a nut and an iron shoe.  There are three purlins, and a "pile" plate is fastened on the rafters above the upper purlin, on which the feet of the short upper rafters are supported. This provides effective ventilation evenly distributed along the whole length of the roof, in lieu of the ordinary louvre-board arrangement.

The choice of one or the other of these designs for a cow-house will necessarily be affected by the position of the yards and of the other buildings at a homestead, but doubtless the double cow-house affords the cheapest accommodation. Where it is possible for a cow-house to occupy

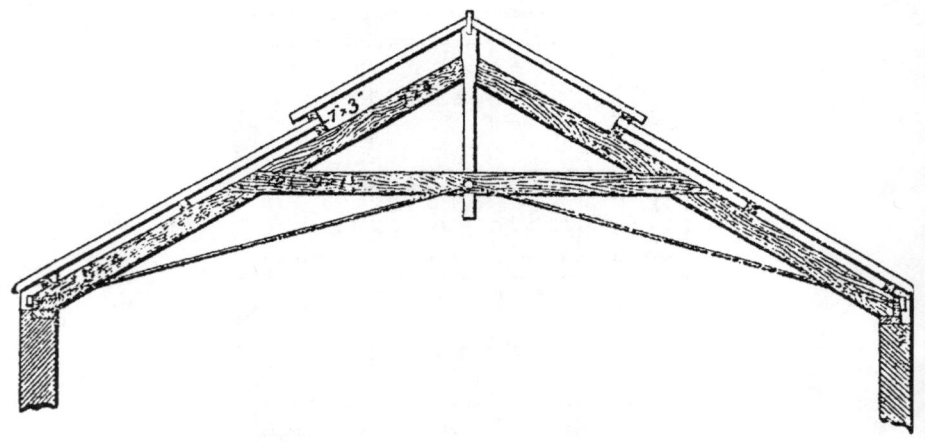

FIG. 12.

a central position between stockyards, as in some of the example plans of homesteads previously given, it will be advisable in the case of a double cow-house to put the feeding passage in the centre, and the dunging passages to adjoin the yards which will receive the manure. On the other hand, if the end only of a cow-house abuts upon a manure yard, it may be desirable to have two entrances for the cows, and a central dunging passage with one exit for the soiled litter. At many homesteads no feeding passage exists in the cow-houses, and where perhaps nothing but uncut hay is given, the absence of this passage would not be felt ; but as it is almost universal now to use chaffed and mixed food, the omission of this convenient means of access to the mangers should be avoided where possible, except perhaps in small structures where it is not so much needed.

Where bricks are reasonable in price, and of near carriage, 9-inch brick walls will probably be the kind selected, as they are well adapted for cow-houses and all single-storey buildings. Walls 14 inches thick are not necessary, although frequently met with, but of course piers of this thickness are required at intervals in 9-inch walls to give support for the principals. Experienced readers may think it unnecessary that such an evident precaution should be pointed out, but as I have seen frequent instances of the omission of these piers, which have resulted in disaster, this must be the excuse for referring to it.

The method of fitting up the interior and other details will be the next subject for consideration.

As modern medical research has apparently justified the imposition of the sanitary laws before referred to upon the owners of cow-houses in respect of the housing of dairy animals, it is clear that we have a factor to consider here which is not forced upon our attention in the case of any other building connected with farm homesteads, except of course as regards dairies, but these are, properly speaking, part of the equipment of farmhouses.

The necessary sanitary efficiency will be attained by the provision of suitable paving, draining, lighting, ventilation, and sufficient area, the last of these points having already been referred to. As regards paving, one naturally turns first to local productions, and in many places various kinds of stones are to be obtained on landed estates for the mere cost of quarrying them. Large stone slabs are undoubtedly the best for the purpose, as there are fewer joints in which liquids can lodge; blocks or cubes of smaller surface area are next in order; then the various stones suitable for rough paving, which are found mostly in gravel and chalk. The best floor is undoubtedly that which combines durability with a surface free from irregularities, and which is impervious to moisture, and these qualities are to be secured by the use of cement concrete, asphalte, or a hard paving brick thoroughly well laid on a proper foundation. The floor which is most efficient from a sanitary point of view is also the most advantageous to the farmer who finds it necessary to economise the use of straw, as a free flow of liquid excreta to the drains results in the soiling of a less quantity of litter; but it is needless to say that the necessity for economy, which is almost always present, must in most instances determine the choice of materials. A damp course to all cow-house walls is desirable, and if the inside of the walls, as well as the woodwork, is tarred occasionally, cleanliness will be promoted; and if means can be devised for flushing the floors with water, it will be very advantageous.

The employment of wood as a paving material is worthy of attention, as the following extracts from the *Transactions* of the Surveyors' Institution will show; but it will not be suited for urban or other cow-houses from which milk is sold, for sanitary reasons. The author of this work and Mr C. J. Mann having introduced the papers for discussion which were referred to in a previous chapter, Mr Squarey (afterwards President of the Institution) said: " It was only a few months ago that, seeing in the timber yard of a large estate of which he had the supervision a lot of timber the boughs and offcuts of elms, oaks, and other varieties of trees, which were practically useless for any other purpose but fuel, it occurred to him that they might be used in place of brick pavement for their large cow-stalls. This had accordingly been done, and the buildings had now been in use for two or three months, and so far the plan had been a success. He regretted that he had not with him the figures showing the actual cost; but he could state that debiting the estate with the timber at about 6d. per cubic foot, there was decided economy in the employment of the wood for the purpose, and it had proved far cheaper than the bricks of the district. There had been no sinking of any part of the pavement, and the moisture kept the timber so effectually swelled that not a drop of it passed down on to the concrete on which it was laid." Mr A. D. Clarke, in his reply upon the discussion on the papers, said: "He wished to add his testimony in favour of the system, although his experiments with wooden flooring had been of a different kind. For the paving of cow-stalls he had used a selection from disused railway sleepers, which were often to be bought at about 1s. each; they were of sufficient length to reach from the manger to the drain channel, 5 inches thick, and seven of them in width would be sufficient for two cow-standings. The warm and even surface which they presented, as compared with stones, was of great advantage, in allowing of much less litter to be used without lessening the comfort of an animal; and no description of flooring could be much cheaper where it could be obtained. On those estates where timber was plentiful, and suitable flooring material scarce, it might be worth while to cut up any rough trees or limbs into planks for this purpose, although they must not be expected to last so long as the sleepers, as these had the advantage of being creosoted."

As regards the feeding passage, not being subjected to so much wear and tear, or to the action of urine from the cows, a floor of well-rammed earth, or of any rough concrete, will be all that is necessary, unless appearances have to be studied, when ordinary building bricks would suffice if carefully laid in sand on a well-rammed surface. But these remarks will not apply to urban districts where an impervious floor is necessary to meet the sanitary requirements for cow-houses in which cows are constantly confined.

The drain-channel being subject to much wear, and liable, if not properly constructed, to get out of order, should always be strongly formed; and, in view of the sanitary requirements referred to, it should carry the liquids

FIG. 13.

to the outside of the buildings, instead of discharging its contents into a cesspit in the inside of the house, which has been more or less a custom hitherto.

Fig. 13 is a sectional illustration of a channel formed of 'bull-nosed" blue Staffordshire bricks, but those of any other manufacture would do equally well provided they were hard enough to stand the wear. The advantage of a channel of this kind is in its 10-inch width of flat surface forming the bottom being adapted for the free passage of a shovel for cleaning it out; but care should be taken in laying the channel that the bed or standing space for the cows should be long enough (not less than 7 feet) to

## Their Construction and Arrangement. 61

allow them to lie down without their extremities overlapping it, as the resulting absence of support to the parts where this precaution is omitted produces abortion in the later period of gestation. It is undesirable also to give more than two or three inches of fall from the manger to the drain.

It has been previously remarked that ample light is of importance in farm buildings, and with glass so cheap as it is objection to its liberal use in cow-houses can scarcely be taken on the ground of economy. Dark interiors are doubtless a premium to imperfect work, and to dirty accumulations in remote corners which an open door sheds no light upon, and they should be condemned accordingly, so far at least as any new buildings are under consideration. The admission of light by the insertion in plain tile roofs of squares of rough plate-glass, or in a pantile roof of glass tiles, is probably the most effective as well as the most economical means to adopt, as in both cases there will be no woodwork to provide or paint, or to perish for the want of paint as is far too often the case, and being in the roof the danger of breakage will be reduced to a minimum. It is quite safe to pronounce in favour of this system in preference to windows, with their continual want of attention and repair ; and in place of the ventilating properties of the window, which would be sacrificed, there should be ventilating bricks inserted in the walls, or ordinary agricultural drain pipes sloping upwards to the interior of the building should be built in at intervals.

However, where windows are preferred, the kind shown by the illustration (Fig. 14) is as much to be recommended as any, and is very superior to many others, not only for cow-houses but for all parts of a homestead. The upper part is glazed with strong rough plate-glass, and the lower fitted with fixed bars, and a sliding framework of bars to cover up the apertures when desired. This kind of window is not likely to get out of order; there is no casement hung to be blown about by wind, and the glass is high enough to be free from risk of breakage by animals. In granaries, and other buildings out of the way of stock, it may sometimes be advisable to have more glass, and in such cases a sash hung on a pivot may be suitable.

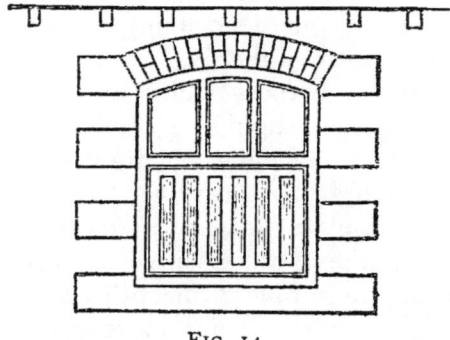

FIG. 14.

As regards doorways frequented by animals, they should not be less than 4 feet wide in the clear, and be hung in halves. Where possible those used for the exit of cows should open into a fold-yard, as the voidance of excreta nearly always takes place when they are untied, and the soiling of roads and passages is thereby avoided. Simplicity of construction is best for all farm building work, on account of repairs often being taken in hand by rough handy workmen about the homesteads; therefore plain strong ledged and braced doors are the best, and they are also the most durable. Framed doors should be avoided, the joints being a source of weakness, and the framework becoming loose from the knocking about in rough weather.

## Their Construction and Arrangement.

The arrangements for effective ventilation of cow-houses may be of the most simple kind. Admission of air can be made in the walls by the ventilating brick or drain-pipe arrangement referred to, with or without the assistance of windows, and its exit from the roof can be obtained by the occasional bedding of a ridge tile on the adjoining ones, or by the use of ventilating ridge tiles. This will be ample for tile roofs, whether plain or pantiled, and in most cases also will suffice for slate coverings, in lieu of the more costly and troublesome louvre-boarded erections at the ridge, which can thus be avoided. But whatever aids are introduced for carrying off vitiated air, the aim should be to obtain the upward current as far as possible without creating a direct draught upon the animals, and therefore all cross currents should be avoided. Small and frequent openings in the roof are preferable to larger outlets, as the down draughts are less, and the distribution of fresh air is more perfect where the exits are smaller than inlets individually, but greater in their collective area.

The sharp angles of all door frames should be chamfered off; and where doors are hung in brickwork, round-nosed bricks should be used, to lessen the risk of knocked down hips and other injuries to the cows. This, and the previously mentioned matters of detail, are not of so trifling a nature as may be imagined, at least not to initiated minds; and it need hardly be said, that directly anything in the shape of bodily ailment occurs, a cow not only ceases to yield profit, but it becomes a source of expense in the treatment required for its restoration to health. Moreover, wherever new work is undertaken, it must not be forgotten that the sanitary inspector is to be reckoned with where milk is sold, or should infectious diseases arise at or near the homestead or in the neighbourhood.

Of mangers there are, as we know, many kinds, each district usually preferring that which is most in use in its own neighbourhood, therefore inquiry is necessary before determining what sort to provide. Some farmers prefer a high manger, others a low one ; but the mode of feeding the cows is more likely than anything else to influence the choice. Where a feeding passage is not required, and the cows are fed on hay or straw and a few whole roots, a couple of planks put about 2 ft. 6 in. from the wall is often

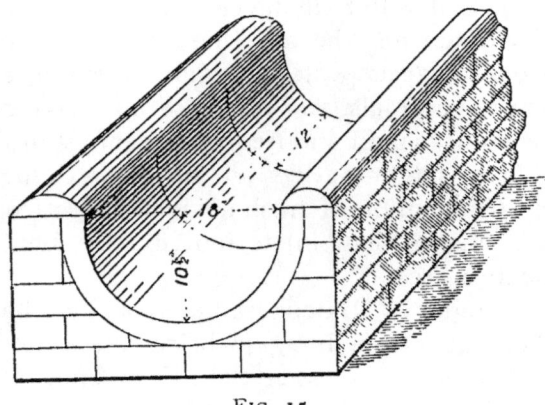

FIG. 15.

all that is needed to form the manger, and the cows are tied to poles fixed to crosspieces of timber above. Room for bulky food is in such cases needed, and it is clear that this may be an economical and effective method of providing it ; but the majority of farmers now feed to a great extent with chaff, cut roots, and cake or meal, and they like a smaller and more perfect trough. Three examples of mangers suited for prepared food are given at Figs. 15, 16, and 17, the first being of half pipes with cement coping, which makes an excellent manger ; the second of manger bricks; and the last of manger blocks of brown earthenware, all being on foundations of brickwork, and suitable for erection either with a feeding passage or against a wall.

In Fig. 16 the bottom and back of the manger is formed with Staffordshire paving bricks or squares (or otherwise good quality building bricks may be substituted); and the front, as shown, is filled in with manger bricks, with a roll on the upper edge to prevent the food being turned out.

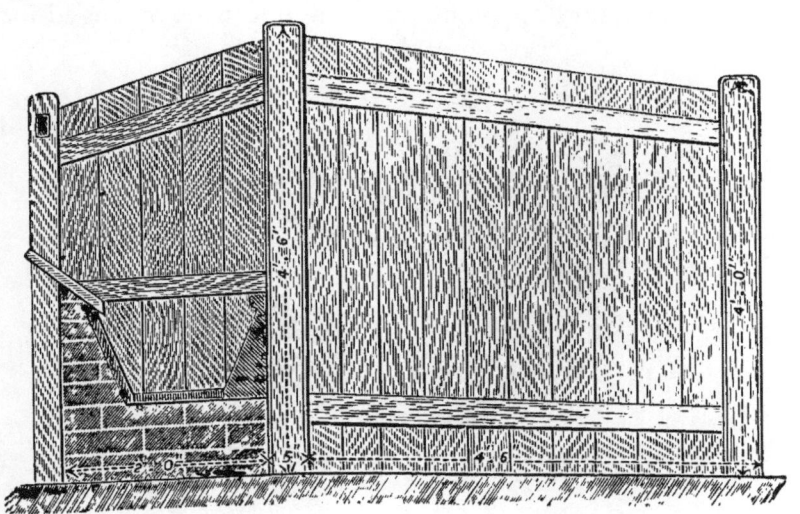

FIG. 16.

This manger stands on a base of three courses of brickwork, and, on the whole, it forms a very durable erection at a moderate cost. There is a sloping board at the back, which serves as a sill for securing the brickwork, as well as to conduct the food from the feeding passage to the manger, this being passed through between the board and the rail, which is shown in section.

E

The last of the three illustrations (Fig. 17) represents a manger of a very superior and costly kind, which, it must be admitted, is very seldom met with except in model buildings and at home farms, where the best appearance is required.  It consists of a front and back of brown glazed earthenware blocks, each about 12 inches in width and in height, with ends and divisions made to match ; and when fixed in cement they also make excellent water-troughs. The width, therefore, of this manger is 2 feet, and it is hardly necessary to point out that it can be arranged for

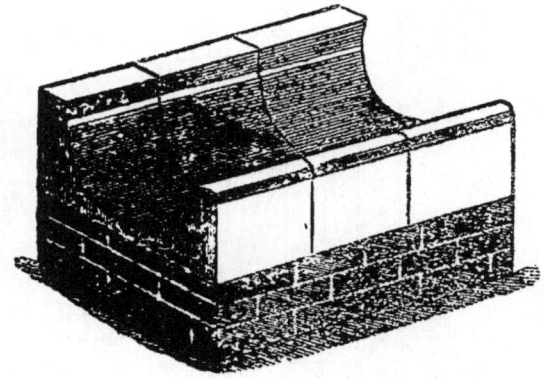

FIG. 17.

taking the food supply in the same manner as shown and described for the preceding figure.  The best height for a manger is no doubt a medium one, say about 1 ft. 9 in. from the ground line to the top of it ; and the backs should always have a sufficient slope to allow of enough space for the horns of animals when feeding.  If this is neglected, imperfectly cleared-out mangers is the result.

Any remarks on the fitting up of cow-houses will not be complete without a reference to the stall divisions,

## Their Construction and Arrangement. 67

or travises as they are sometimes called. The custom of some particular districts dispenses with them, but generally speaking they are required, and the advantages attending their adoption are of some weight. At Fig. 16 an illustration of a stall division is given. A post 4 ft. 6 in. high is placed close against the front of the manger called the headpost, and another, 4 ft. high, 4 ft. 6 in. to the rear of it, called the heelpost. Into these are mortised top and bottom rails for receiving the boarding, which is nailed upon one side only; and a slighter post is placed at the back of the manger, in the feeding passage, to receive two short rails taking that part of the boards forming the division over the manger, which extends downwards to the bottom of it to keep the food in its proper place. Other methods of construction are of course met with; occasionally posts are grooved, and boards inserted horizontally in them, which are afterwards braced together; but when thus formed the divisions are obviously more difficult to repair. Simplicity of construction is undoubtedly best, and if the upright boarding as shown in the illustration is followed out, the utmost repair that can be required after some years of use will be the occasional nailing on of a board, which any man can do. Occasionally one sees the division made with four rails instead of boards, which answers well, and promotes the free circulation of air, which is now considered so desirable. All sharp edges of posts and rails should be slightly chamfered off, and the bottom rail be kept some inches off the floor for its better preservation.

The headpost by the manger will serve for tying up a cow on each side by means of two $\frac{3}{4}$-inch iron rods, 2 feet long, being bolted through the post, having iron rings attached for sliding up and down for affixing the neck chains of the cows. The first use of stall divisions is here apparent, as this saves posts which would otherwise be required for the purpose of securing the animals; but perhaps the principal reason of their adoption is that, when placed at proper intervals, cows are free from disturbance, and prevented from turning round and fouling their bed. This they are otherwise very apt to do, and after having laid down a good deal of time is taken up in cleaning the animals before milking can, or ought, to take place.

In the remarks made previously in connection with the ground-plan illustrations of cow-houses, the distance apart of the stall divisions was discussed, therefore no reference here on this point is needed. Cow-house accommodation, however, can hardly be said to be complete without one or more

### LOOSE BOXES AND CALF-HOUSES.

A box for calving, or for a sick cow, is a very desirable addition, either to the cow-house itself, or attached to some other part of the homestead. It ought to contain at least 100 superficial feet of area, and be parted off, if in the cow-house, by a division not less than 6 feet high, and free from draughts. At Fig. 9 in a previous chapter is shown an arrangement for making a box at will out of the two end stalls of a cow-house, which the author has frequently adopted from motives of economy, the box thus formed being also useful occasionally for calves, or for storing hay or straw for daily use. The stall division is continued to the drain-channel, and a wicket is hung to a post at the back wall, which shuts on to the heelpost of the stall. Other convenient positions for calving boxes are indicated on the plans of example homesteads previously given.

A place for calves is the natural accompaniment to every cow-house, and no other class of young farming stock

## Their Construction and Arrangement. 69

suffers so much if not properly housed, as scouring, followed speedily by loss of life, often takes place where a clean and dry bed is not maintained. Generally speaking, a number of calves are allowed to run together in one box, which answers very well for rearing purposes; but when they are to be fed for the butcher the quieter they are kept the better, and for this purpose some farmers prefer a number of small enclosures or pens for the purpose of confining them singly, and in darkness almost, to induce complete

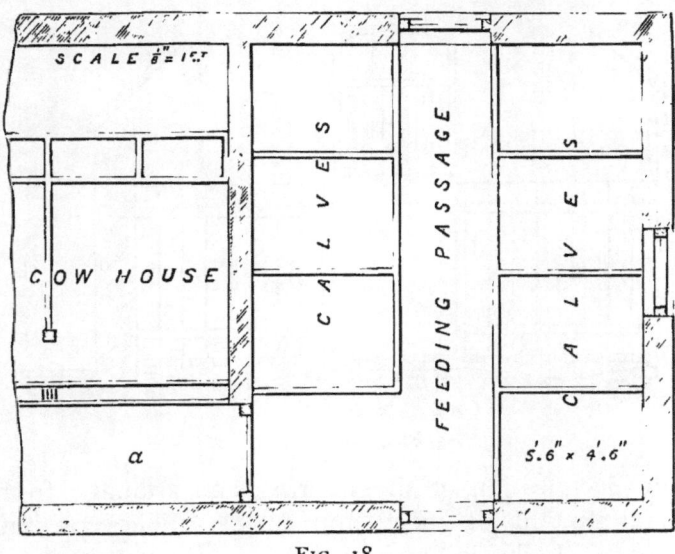

FIG. 18.

repose. If the former method is resorted to, about 30 feet of area for each calf is sufficient; but if the latter is needed, 25 feet is all that is required, this being about the size of each of the seven compartments shown in Fig. 18. These are provided with access by means of a passage leading from that at the rear of the cow-standings in the cow-house to which it is attached.

Granting that it is correct, as most practical farmers assert, that fattening calves thrive best in semi-darkness, it must be admitted that those about to be reared require light, sun, air, and space, in order that the frame which hereafter is to carry its complement of beef should receive early development without any check whatever. So far, therefore, the qualifications for suitable quarters are indicated, but the prevention of the evils attending scour is perhaps the most important point of all. This is involved

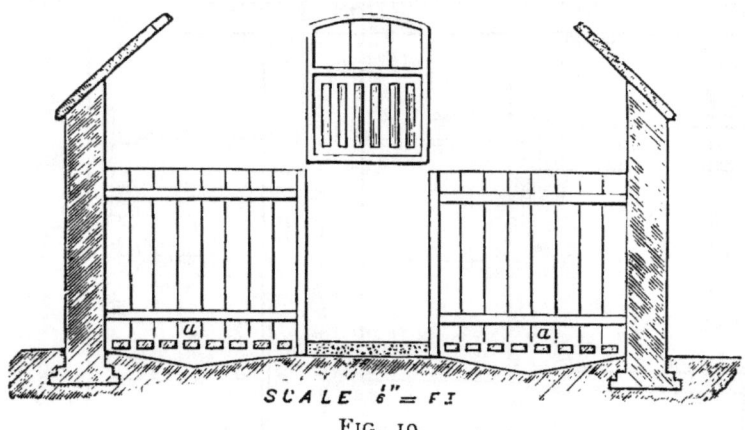

FIG. 19.

mainly in the question of site, flooring, and drainage, from the builder's point of view, and in cleanliness on the farmer's part. If the soil and situation of the calf-house is not naturally damp and cold, calves will usually thrive if placed on an evenly paved brick floor, sloping to a drain in or outside the house—that is if they are properly attended to and supplied with dry litter; but if the conditions of the site are the reverse, it is absolutely necessary, if scouring is to be avoided, that "sparred flooring" should be put down above the paving, as shown in section at *a*, *a*, in Fig. 19, which is a sectional drawing of the previous figure. The boards are about 4 by 1½, with 1¼-inch apertures (through which solids as well as liquids will pass), and nailed on ledges, in sections of a convenient size for taking up when required. Where necessary wooden bearers or sleepers can be laid to take the bearings; and the floors below being sloped or dished, all the moisture will run away. This kind of flooring should always be made to be removable, as when the house is not required for calves it may be useful for cows that would be too heavy for the flooring.

The divisions forming the pens in Fig. 18 may be either of 4½-inch brickwork, close boarding, or paling; and the fitting up of places for calves will be comprised in a small wooden manger being fastened to one of the walls, and a light hay-rack. The latter, however, is frequently dispensed with.

It may not be out of place to mention here, in reference to the need of boarded floors, that the author recently refused to put in a boarded floor for two newly constructed calf-houses on a large farm, preferring, as he told the tenant, to wait and see whether the brick floors provided would ensure freedom from scour; but the tenant was so sure (judging from his former experience at the same homestead) the evil would appear, that he would not run the risk, and laid a bottom of faggots on the bricks as a preventive measure!

## CHAPTER VI.

### FEEDING STALLS AND BOXES.

THERE are few farms at which cattle are kept—whether purely dairy farms or otherwise—that do not occasionally produce a few fat animals. Store stock may be selling badly, or there may be a surplusage of roots to be consumed, or for some other reason the manufacture of beef is now and then undertaken, therefore it is desirable to have some sort of provision for feeding cattle on these occupations (as well as on those at which it is a recognised practice), whether it takes the form of stalls, of boxes, or of yards. Every farmer is compelled, unless he is prepared to quit the ranks of his profession a loser, to take advantage now of any circumstance which may yield a suitable return, or otherwise prevent a loss, therefore the occasional departure from usual practice is necessary.

We have for fattening stock four classes of structures to deal with—stalls, boxes, open yards, and covered yards. First, as regards stalls, little requires to be said, as any properly constructed cow-house, such as those indicated at Figs. 9, 10, and 11, is equally suitable for fattening purposes. Where, however, cow-houses have roughly constructed mangers of wood, such as are used where dairy cows are fed chiefly upon hay, such mangers are ill adapted for the use of the prepared foods usually given to stall-fed stock, and one of those shown at Figs. 15, 16, or 17 would be much better adapted for the purpose.

It will not be out of place here to refer to the question of the comparative cost of building stalls, boxes, and yards for a given number of animals requiring to be fed, and to the reasons for the adoption of the systems respectively. Stalls are doubtless more used than either of the latter, and this for several reasons, the principal, perhaps, being that an existing cow-house not wholly in use answers the purpose without any fresh outlay in building. Again, as regards cost, if new buildings are to be specially erected, say for 20 head of cattle, stalls will be cheaper than boxes, and probably only about the same cost as two yards with sheds for ten head each, if these are properly walled in ; the proper superficial area for one animal in a stall, including the share of the passage before and behind for feeding and dunging out, being about 65 ft. ; in a box, 100 ft. ; and in a yard, 160 ft. Again, some farmers prefer stalls, because the dung is daily thrown out into the yards and mixed with that from the stables, the whole being consolidated with the tread of younger cattle, to which any food left in the mangers is also given. Dung thus made is more useful, being of uniform quality. On the other hand, the advocates of box-feeding claim for it a great superiority in the manure produced when it is allowed to accumulate a foot or two thick under the animals, instead of being thrown out on the yards to be alternately washed out by the rain and bleached by the sun ; and this superiority cannot be denied, as it is generally the case that a liberal use of cake and other concentrated foods is made which is supposed to add largely to the value of the manure, and to make its better preservation more necessary. Fig. 20 represents a portion of a cattle-house having a double row of boxes for one beast, 10 ft. by 8 ft. each, supplied from a central feeding passage; and it shows the position of two wings containing larger boxes for pairs, 12 ft. by 11 ft. each, with a feeding passage on one side. The latter, however, would require to be a little larger for two matured animals of a large breed. A section across this building is shown at Fig. 21 on a larger scale. The width inside is

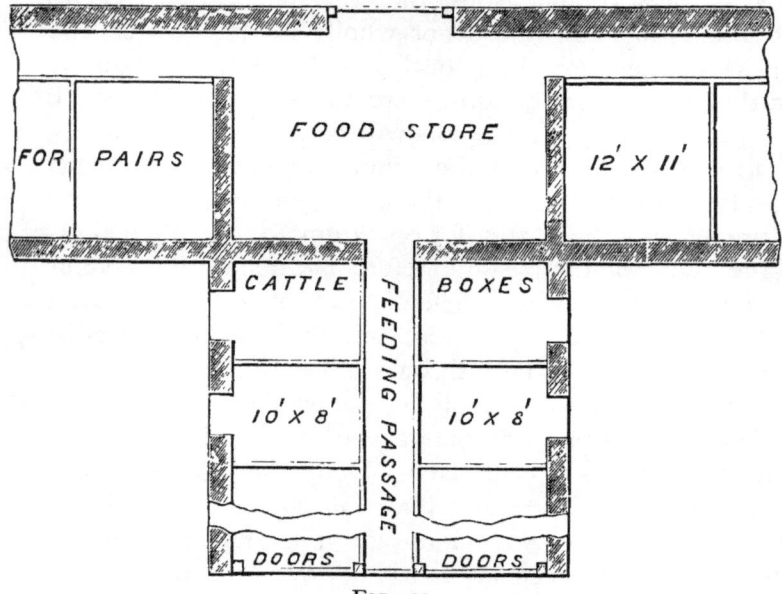

FIG. 20.

25 ft., and doors are provided to each box opening into a yard for general use; but to facilitate the removal of manure, which it will be seen is from 2 to 3 ft. deep, doors are placed at the end of the building, wide enough to allow carts to be backed in and loaded up direct. The gate-like divisions are removable upwards as the manure accumulates, and are taken out altogether to admit the carts,

## Their Construction and Arrangement. 75

being fastened by means of iron pins, shown at *a*, *b*, into timber built into the walls, or otherwise posts. The box nearest the door is cleared first, to admit the cart to the second, the work proceeding thus until all are emptied.

When boxes are constructed for cattle they should, to attain their full value and convenience, be built somewhat on the lines here advocated. There is also another advan-

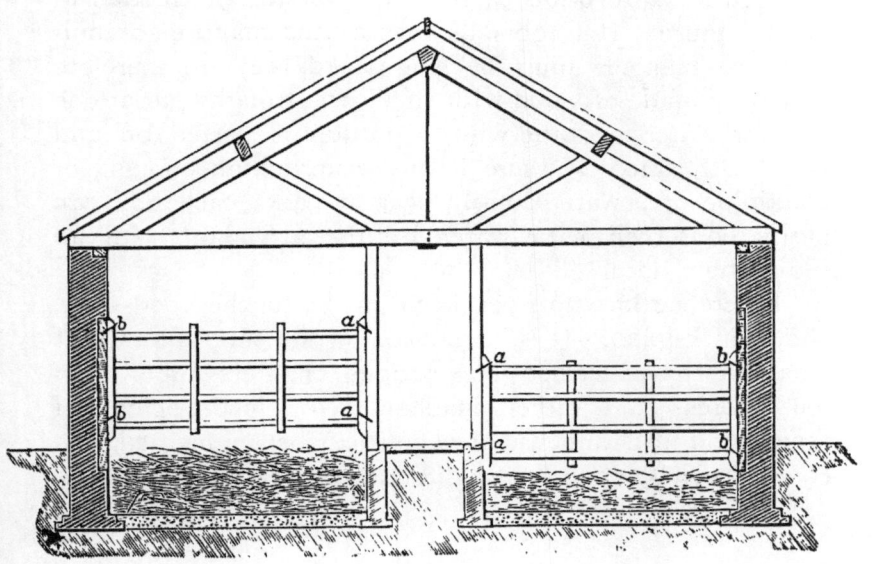

FIG. 21.

tage when removable divisions are used, as if all are taken away the building for the time being makes an excellent covered yard for young stock, protecting them from the weather and allowing them space for the necessary exercise for the development of their frames. In fact, owing to the varied uses they can be made to serve, boxes are gradually becoming more popular.

As regards other details in the fitting up of boxes, it will be advisable for the post of the divisions to be secured to the tie-beams (these being lighter in consequence) for the sake of strength ; also that a proper supply of light and ventilation be obtained, although these matters are not of such importance as in the case of dairy cow-houses. No system of drainage is necessary, as all liquids will be required for absorption by the straw for the production of good manure. It is obvious that as the manure accumulates the mangers must be heightened, they are therefore generally made of wood with small iron troughs put at one end for water, or otherwise a portion is parted off and lined with zinc. If there is any cistern high enough, or standpipe of a water supply near at hand, each box can easily be served with water by the attendant with an indiarubber hose.

Reference has not yet been made to the food-store, shown in Fig. 20. It is introduced on the supposition that what we have termed in previous chapters the "main food-stores" are either inadequate or inconvenient of access, and if its dimensions require to be augmented, this could easily be done in any direction.

## CHAPTER VII.

### OPEN STOCKYARDS.

AT every homestead where stock is kept one or more yards are required, according to the extent of the farm. In old-fashioned homesteads the yards are nearly always too large, the ill effects of which are apparent in the distribution of the manure in a thin layer, with too much surface exposed to the deleterious effects of the elements. Another evil in these old yards often exists in the shape of roadways running across them, which either have to be cleaned up at a considerable expenditure of workmen's time, or otherwise they remain an intolerable nuisance. Again, the surface of many yards was either originally ill constructed, or otherwise has been allowed to wear into holes, into which water drains from the adjacent ground, thus producing discomfort to animals and deterioration of manure, and the necessity for the use of large quantities of straw, part of which might be eaten by the cattle or sold with advantage. In fact, at the present time the low price of grain renders it a matter of necessity on many farms to sell a portion of straw. This need not be considered evidence of bad farming, as was at one time the case, as whenever the low-priced grain is consumed on the farm, or artificial feeding stuffs are purchased in proportion to such sales, fertility is maintained.

Such being the chief evils of ill-constructed yards, in

noting them the key is supplied in a great measure for making them in a proper and serviceable manner.

As regards size, each beast will require about 160 superficial feet of area, not less, and, of the surface occupied by the yard, about one-third should be covered over to form a shelter shed, the shed being fairly wide, say 15 ft., to enable the cattle to get away from driving storms. But we may

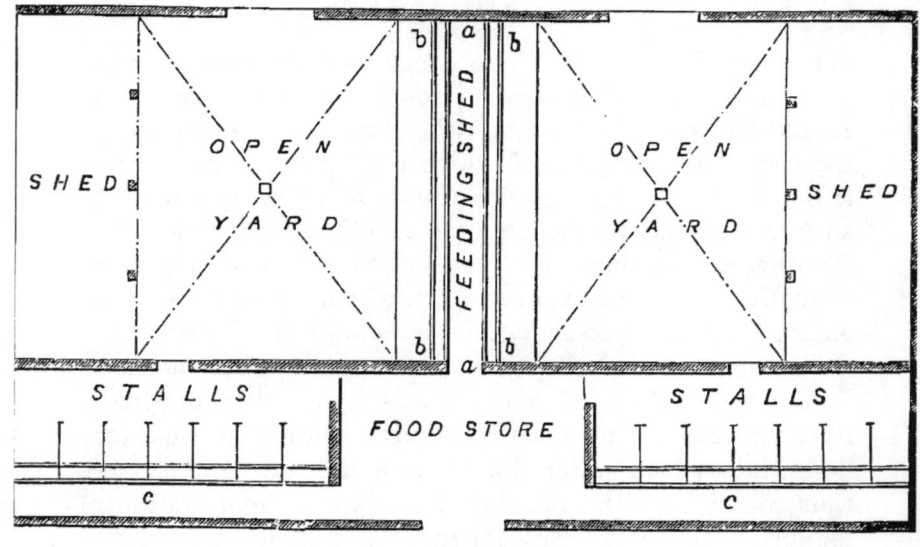

FIG. 22.

here refer to the illustration, Fig. 22. The yards are 45 ft. wide, of which the sheds occupy 15 ft.; and in the example plans of homesteads already given several other forms of yards are shown.

The feeding of cattle in yards should be arranged with a view of despatch. Some farmers like to have the mangers in the sheds; while others prefer "cribs" standing in the open, in order that the daily supply of clean litter

## Their Construction and Arrangement. 79

for the sheds may be economised by the absence of the treading in of the same, which arises when cattle are feeding from the mangers. Where a small extra expense is not objected to, a shed with a central feeding passage communicating directly with the food-store, as at *a a* in Fig. 22, is an excellent plan to adopt, allowing as it does in this case just sufficient space for a manger and shelter at *b b* on each side for the cattle. This arrangement is further illustrated in section at Fig. 23, the roof being

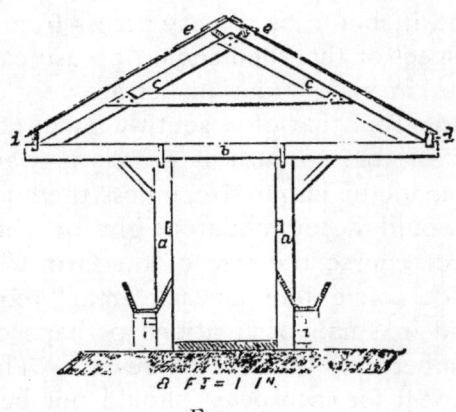

FIG. 23.

constructed cheaply of corrugated iron : *a, a,* are posts each side of the feeding passage about 9 ft. apart; *b* is a light tie-beam ; *c, c,* are rafters at the same distance ; and *d, d,* and *e, e,* are the eaves and ridge timbers for fastening the iron upon. The usual posts to support the roof at the eaves are dispensed with, these being in the feeding passage to support the rails over the mangers, which form the fence to keep the animals out of the passage. A cheaper roof could scarcely be constructed, as there are no rafters beyond the principals, and the whole of the timbers may be of the lightest description—deal battens 6 in. by 2½ in. will be sufficient throughout.

A well-constructed and properly placed stockyard is doubtless one of the most useful structures on a farm, but there are several points besides those referred to which remain to be noted. To ensure economy and good shelter, advantage should be taken of any existing buildings available for forming one or more sides of the enclosure. Where possible, it should have cow-house or stable doors opening into it for receiving the manure daily removed therefrom ; and it should be of easy access from the straw-store. The aspect of the shed should be as near south as possible, except in such situations as are very exposed to prevailing winds from that of a south-west direction, when it might be desirable to turn it more eastward. Yards should not be made of larger size, unless there is a special reason, than would accommodate eight or ten full-sized animals; but of course the size of the farm will regulate this to a considerable extent, as each " rear" requires to be kept apart, and in small occupations perhaps only six or even a less number may be annually reared. The space of 160 superficial feet for each beast should not be exceeded, even if large quantities of manure from the surrounding buildings are to be cast into the yard, as space can be provided for this by excavating the surface, thereby allowing an accumulation of manure to a greater depth, and assisting also its preservation for the reasons already stated.

The eaves of the shelter sheds should not be higher than is necessary to allow for the accumulation of manure, or their efficiency will be impaired—about 8 feet from the ground will be sufficient. The surface of the yard should be dished towards the centre, to a cesspool covered with a strong grating, a drain from which should be laid to carry away the liquid to the desired point; if not dished to the centre, to any other more suitable point.

Very little requires to be said of the fitting up of cattle-yards, as this is comprised almost solely in the manger accommodation. If no feeding passage is given, the manger should be placed as conveniently as possible for the supply of food, as the crossing of wet yards in winter with a basketful of food at a time is a sorrowful proceeding. A few openings in a wall, protected with shutters, for passing in the food, is often found to be a good substitute for a feeding passage, as by this means a truck-load at a time of food may be taken from the store; and it is by attention to details of this kind that the usefulness of a structure is promoted, and time—which is money—saved.

Gates for stockyards should be 10 ft. wide, not 9 ft. as is often the case. Walls about 5 ft. high are preferable to rails, for many reasons, where the site is unsheltered, if bricks are not too costly; and the eaves of all adjoining buildings should be spouted, and the water carried off by drains. A drinking trough of iron is a decided advantage where it can be suitably supplied with water, particularly in the case of yards for fattening cattle.

The foregoing remarks are intended more particularly to apply to new erections; but in everyday practice on agricultural properties the improvement of homesteads by additional shedding most frequently presents itself. In such cases the problem will be, of course, to make the best of the general surroundings. Tenants will frequently ask for a new yard, to be placed upon additional ground; whereas the amount of space enclosed by the existing buildings is often found to be ample, if it is put into shape, divided by a fence, and a shed, lean-to or otherwise, erected. Custom has induced them to think that these large yards are necessary, but it will be better to apply the test of allowing 160 feet of area for each beast, and not to exceed that amount, otherwise compactness will be sacrificed, extra labour will be incurred in carrying on the work at the homestead, and the manure will be injured.

## CHAPTER VIII.

### COVERED YARDS.

THE covering in of yards for cattle is of comparatively recent introduction. Their advantages have been fairly discussed, and as a rule those farmers who have had them, provided they were properly constructed, would not wish to be without them; yet it must be admitted that practical men are not all in favour of them.

The opinions of the judges of the Farm Homestead designs exhibited at the Royal Agricultural Society's Show at Kilburn, in 1870, are of interest. They state that "the most striking feature in the exhibition of farm plans, viewed as a whole, was the fact that the covering of stock and manure was the object most frequently aimed at—a large number of the exhibitors adopting permanent roofs for fold-yards, and, in some cases, for corn, straw, and haystacks." Whether this supply of covered yards represented a corresponding demand on the part of the occupiers of land, or otherwise, is a question we should be glad to see definitely settled. It appeared, however, from the list of competitors, that about one-half of them were land agents, who might be expected to be in touch with the tenants and give reflection to their opinion. The judges proceeded to say: "There is no doubt whatever that the principle of protecting from the weather both animals and manure has gained ground considerably since the Society offered prizes for plans of farm buildings thirty years ago. The economy of warmth in feeding both growing and fattening stock, and the value of straw for fodder as well as litter, have both tended to the covering of fold-yards—a step which is likely to be more appreciated as our population increases, and agriculture undergoes those changes which best promote the increased production of winter-fed meat. It is difficult to say which of the two characters of stock— matured beasts preparing for the butcher, or growing steers and heifers which it is intended to turn into pastures during the summer—do best under cover during the winter. Experience in a majority of cases has contradicted the assertion that open yards with shelter sheds are more healthy than covered yards for young animals. It is found to be hardly possible to make any animals too snug and warm if the accommodation is associated with proper ventilation, though many tenants of tillage farms producing a large quantity of straw prefer open fold-yards, on the simple ground that straw is more quickly consumed. It has been advanced with great truth that farmyard manure made under a roof, owing to its dryness and want of solidity, loses a great part of the solidity it should hold, and that its fertilising powers are thereby much reduced; but experience has proved that this dry and light condition is due rather to the wasteful use of straw as litter, where the obligation to consume it on the premises prevails, than to any other cause."

The question of covered yards was also the subject of considerable discussion at the meeting of the Members of the Surveyors' Institution, in 1883, which was referred to in an earlier article. Several eminent and practical land agents on that occasion placed their opinions on record.

Mr F. Chancellor, who has had a very extensive experience, having erected from forty to fifty covered homesteads during the last thirty-five years, said that, " after a good deal of thought and experience, he did not think there was any homestead equal to a covered homestead." Mr Tuckett, from an estimate he had made, found " that a cubic yard of manure taken out of a covered yard was worth at least twice as much as one taken from a well-constructed open yard, and far more than twice as much as one made in a badly constructed yard." Mr W. J. Beadel (Vice-President of the Institution), who gave the results of a long experience, as a land agent and as an agriculturist, of their use at his own homestead, summed up their advantages as follows :—" In the first place, they were most economical ; secondly, stock never did so well as under buildings where they were protected from the elements ; and thirdly, one load of cake-fed manure under a covered yard was equal to three or four loads produced in an uncovered yard." He considered, however, that the coats of young stock kept in covered yards got thin, and consequently great care should be taken in turning them out in spring. His experience was that it was best at first to " turn them into an open yard in the daytime and back into the covered yard at night ; the next fortnight, to turn them into a field close by the homestead in the daytime, and bring them back into the open yard at night ; after which they could be turned out into the pastures without risk of injury to their health." Mr Beadel also stated that he had carried out this system for some years, and had not lost a single animal from it. It would certainly be difficult to devise a more rational mode of treatment than this ; the animal frame is protected from waste by exposure during the winter months, as it should be ; and it is judiciously inured, step by step, in the spring, to the hardier state of existence necessary for outlying beasts. This is done at no expense, and with very little trouble ; and the system must commend itself very favourably to those who use these yards for growing stock. Mr Martin thought that yards wholly covered were to be preferred for fattening stock only, and young stock under one year old ; while he gave it as his opinion that the economy to be obtained by feeding growing beasts in them would not be sufficient to cover the cost of interest on the roofing. Having been agent for 50,000 acres of land for some years without having been asked to put up anything beyond open yards with good wide sheds, he did not think there was much to be claimed for those wholly covered ; and he was satisfied that in his own county at least many farmers were well able to judge what was best for stock. Here we have one important dissentient to their general use for stock ; but Mr G. D. Yeomans' experience in the north of England was quite opposed to this, as it appears from his statement—" that he knew of five or six estates in the north where landlords had put up covered sheds on this plan whenever farms required new buildings, and in several cases the old open yards had been converted into covered yards "—that the tenantry in that district created a considerable demand for them. At the summing up of this important discussion, the President, Mr E. Ryde, said " he was justified, he thought, in saying that the general tone of the discussion seemed to show that covered yards were preferred to open yards. He had found from thirty-five years of experience of covered yards, that there was no advantage to be compared to the housing of young stock under cover, quite apart from fattening stock."

We have now referred at considerable length to the

## Their Construction and Arrangement. 87

opinions of some of the best authorities as to the advantages of these yards, and there can be no doubt that if it were not for their expense they would be much more extensively in use. In making alterations to a homestead, however, the extra cost attending the introduction of a completely roofed-in yard may be more imaginary than real, provided that some cheap material, such as corrugated iron, is used, and that some allowance is made for the general utility of a large covered area at a homestead. We have seen covered yards used for housing the straw from the first day or two's threshing, before the cattle are brought in from the pastures; for sheltering stock on hot summer days to be free from the attacks of flies, and turned out at night to graze; and for horses, pigs, and implements.

In order to reduce the expense of the yards to a minimum, one of the main objects is to secure, so far as possible, the walls without outlay, which may be done wholly or partly in new homesteads by forming suitably sized enclosures in the arrangement of the stables, cowhouses, &c., for the purpose; and at existing homesteads, by taking advantage of such opportunities as may be found to exist in respect of the buildings already standing, or to be erected, as they frequently lend themselves to an economical method of construction for a covered yard.

There is a common idea amongst those persons who have had no experience of these yards, that one or both ends should be open, or partially open, for ventilation; but there could be no greater error. Fatting, and sometimes store, stock are kept in ordinary houses with no further ventilation than that afforded by the doors, windows, and ridge, and a covered yard may be constructed on somewhat similar principles. Draughty erections cannot be too much condemned, and I have seen cases where the gables have been left open, in which the stock would have been better off in an ordinary comfortable open yard with the usual shelter. Ventilation should, if possible, be secured from openings at or near the eaves and the ridge, with some means of regulating it, as shown in the illustrations, Figs. 24 and 25. The first of these shows a method which has proved successful in use, of placing a corrugated iron roof of flat sheets on timbers over a yard enclosed by buildings on three sides. Pillars were carried up at intervals, shown at *a*, on a cow-house wall, 10 feet apart, to support one end of the principals, the other ends being inserted in the walls of a barn, *b*. The span is 32 feet, which is perhaps as wide as a kingpost roof can be serviceably adapted, even for so light a covering as iron. The principal rafters are tapered, and of course no common rafters are needed, the iron being fastened to light purlins, and the ridge capping is elevated and supported on brackets *c, c*, for the purpose of ventilation, which is thereby secured at the least cost. There is no lead gutter where the roof abuts upon the barn, the eaves of the iron being about 6 inches from it and 4½-inch iron guttering fixed, supported by the principals and wall stays, which is inexpensive and easily cleaned out. The total cost of such a roof as this need not exceed about 5s. per yard of ground covered ; and when the iron requires renewal, at present prices this should be done for 2s. 6d. a yard. It ought, however, to be serviceable, although not so durable as tiles or slates, for twenty years at least, and the timbers would require no renewal. A curved iron roof such as described in a subsequent chapter would be suitable instead of this one of flat sheets of iron, but it would be rather more costly.

Fig. 25 is an illustration showing the sectional outline of a series of roofs at a covered homestead such as that designed at Fig. 1. It has especial reference to the circulation of air through the area of the roofs, whereby louvre boarding in the ridge is dispensed with, as explained in the remarks appended to the homestead design. A glance at Fig. 12 in a former chapter will show the details of the roof timbers applicable to the outlines of Fig. 25, which are adapted for slate, corrugated iron, and for some of the improved forms of pantiles, which are much lighter than plain or flat tiles. The latter, on account of their weight, are not so well adapted for wide spans.

The question of roofs and roofing material is such a wide one, that it is hardly possible within the limits of this work to do justice to it, but some further information on the subject is given in a later chapter. We may remark, however, that experience has proved that it is better to cover in a yard if possible with one span than with two, as the intervening posts necessary are generally found in the way, and the single span is more economical if properly carried out. If, however, this should exceed, for slates or iron, more than 35 feet, or for tiles more than 32 feet, a more elaborate and substantially constructed description of principals will be required; and consequently the width of yard to be covered should be kept to such minimum dimensions as are consistent with the circumstances.

Roofs constructed entirely of wood—an example of which is given in a later chapter—doubtless answer very well, if the material is creosoted; but it seems questionable whether they can be put up at a less cost than those of iron. A ton of 24-inch gauge corrugated iron, at £12 per ton, will cover about 162 yards, which is about 1s. 6d. per yard, or 16s. 6d. per square. This would be nearly double the price of the cheapest kind of boarding; but the latter would require purlins fixed more frequently for support, and the

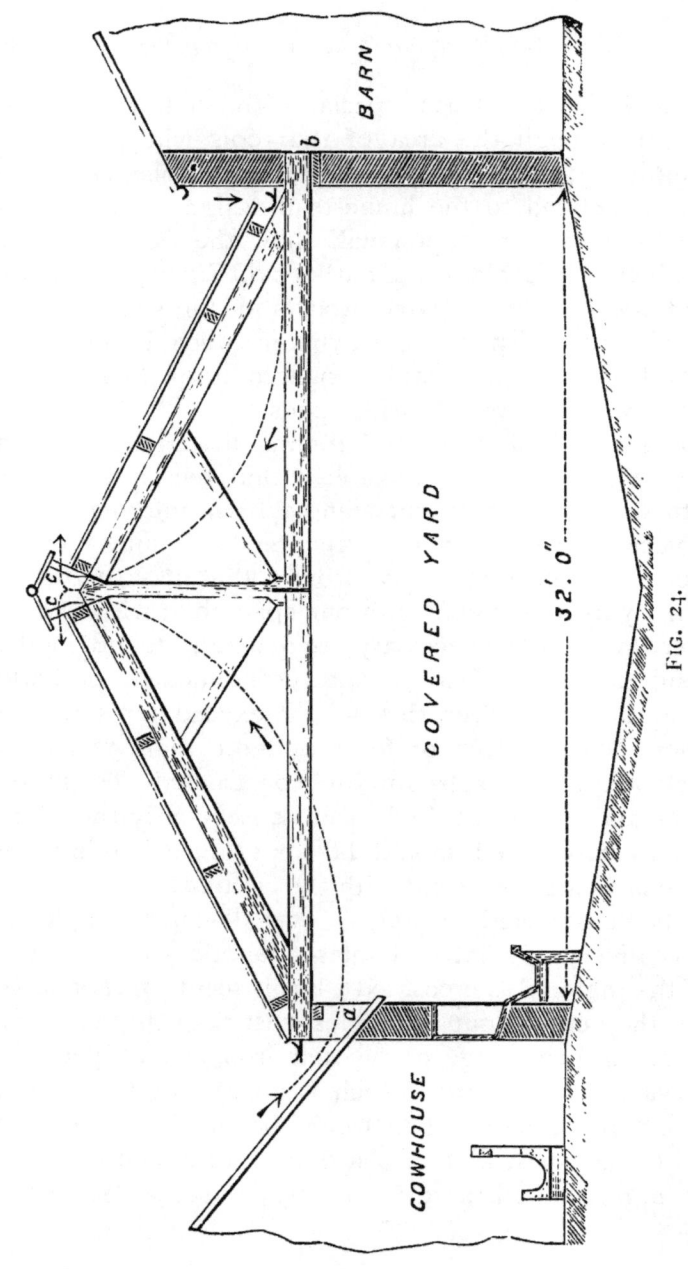

Fig. 24.

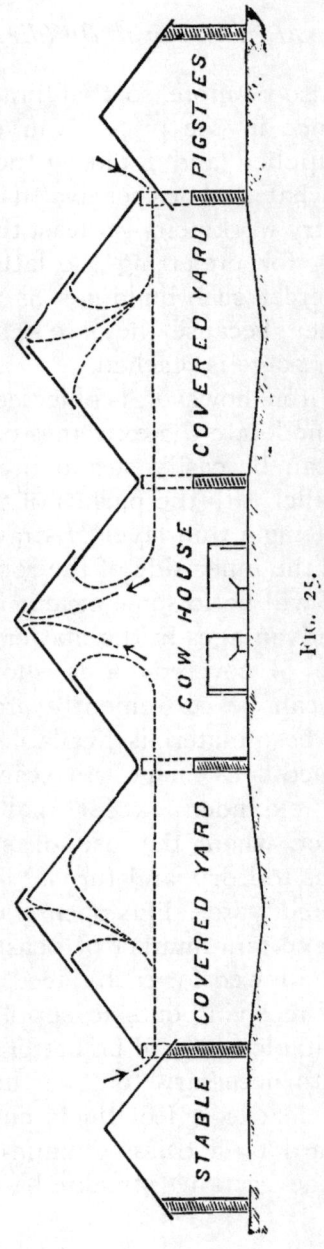

Fig. 25.

labour would also be more, so that practically there would be little difference in the price. Curved corrugated roofs, such as are supplied and fixed by the manufacturers, are however, somewhat more expensive than flat sheeted roofs put up by country workmen,—at least this is my experience, and one reason for preferring the latter; it is also more satisfactory to erect such buildings as are within the scope of local workmen, because they are more easily dealt with when the repair stage is reached.

Corrugated iron, however, is objected to by many people, as it does not moderate the extremes of heat and cold; but this difficulty can be easily surmounted by running some light wires parallel with the purlins of the roof about a foot apart, and inserting a thin layer of straw between the wires and the iron in the inner side of the roof. The comfort of a thatched roof will be to some extent in this way attained, without its disadvantages in the matter of repair.

The surface of covered yards should be paved with stones if they can be conveniently procured, otherwise a coating of the best materials available should be put on and well rammed. Drainage will scarcely be necessary if all liquids are excluded except that passing from the animals; in fact, where the use of straw is liberal, the manure becomes too dry, and turns "fire-fanged," as it is termed. Covered yards, like open yards, constructed to accommodate a certain number of beasts (about 160 feet of area should be allowed for each), need not be enlarged for the purpose of receiving outside supplies of manure from cow-houses or stables; it will be better to excavate to any reasonable depth necessary to take the addition. I have seen manure 4 feet to 5 feet thick, cut out of the centre of a covered yard by a trussing knife—splendid stuff, resembling (in the section) streaky bacon, and for which "hungry" land would be as grateful as a hungry man for the other.

Before concluding the remarks upon these yards, it would not be out of place to quote the following lines upon the principle of giving warmth and shelter to animals from Dr Cameron's book on "The Chemistry of Food." He says: "The bodies of animals are heated masses of matter, and are subject to the ordinary laws of *radiation*. Every substance radiates its heat, and receives in return a portion of that emitted from surrounding bodies. If two bodies of unequal temperature be placed near each other, the warmer of the two will radiate a portion of its heat to the colder, and will receive some of the heat of the latter in return; but as the warmer body will emit more heat than it will receive, the result will be that after a time, the length of which will depend upon the nature of the bodies, both will acquire the same temperature. The philosophy of the *clothing* of men, and the *sheltering* of the lower animals, is now evident. It is not only that heat should be developed within the body, but also that its wasteful expenditure should be prevented."

## CHAPTER IX.

### STABLES.

THE value of good cart horses, and the importance to their owners of maintaining them in a healthy and vigorous condition, equal to the strain of hard work, are sufficient reasons for giving due attention to their accommodation at the homestead; and it will be evident that, possessing a higher physical organisation than any other animals on the farm, horses are in consequence more prone to suffer from ignorance or neglect in their treatment than any kind of farming stock.

In dealing with the question of sheltering horses, regard must first be had to the custom of the district, which, strange though it may appear, varies to the extent of diametrical opposition. In some parts of the eastern counties a stable would almost appear to be a superfluity, or at least merely a place for baiting and cleaning horses, as they are frequently turned out at night in a yard all the year round; and such is their indifference to the state of the weather, that I have seen them standing in a snowstorm not caring even to avail of the shelter of the shed provided in the yard. And experience proves that horses so conditioned are quite healthy, and equal to all the demands put upon them. On the other hand, in the Midlands, and northwards, a warm stable is considered indispensable for winter quarters; and on the principle that warmth is equivalent to a certain amount of food, the practice is sound and unobjectionable, if not carried to extremes, and proper ventilation is given. However, the more tender habit of body which is thereby induced, is evidenced by the use of the loin cloths so often seen on horses in hard weather in these districts.

There is no valid objection to be taken to either system of management, provided it is intelligently and properly applied; but this much may be said of the practice of shutting up farm horses in a stable during long winter nights, for ten hours at a time, that if foulness of atmosphere is not avoided by proper paving and ventilation, evil influences in some form will be at work. Impaired vision and affections of the eye, and colds attended with an undue amount of fever, are often induced by defects of this kind.

Stables should be placed as near as possible to the cart-shedding, for obvious reasons, and it is desirable that the horses should have access to them without crossing yards occupied by stock. Three forms of fitting up the interior are shown by the illustrations, Figs 26, 27, and 28, the first being that in most general use. It will be seen that in each case the horses are separately stalled, which is the safer plan, although sometimes the stalls are omitted. The width of a stall should never be less than 6 feet, and the width of the stable requires to be 17 feet, and disposed of as follows:—Rack and manger, 2 feet; stall and drain-channel, 9 ft. 6 in.; passage at rear, 5 ft. 6 in., which will afford room for a small corn-chest or harness pegs behind the stalls. These dimensions are ample, but not excessive, and anything less would result in inconvenience either to horse or attendant. It is very seldom that boxes are required for all the horses on a farm, but it is desirable to have at least one in a stable, or near by it (for cases of foaling or sickness), such as that shown in Fig. 26, or those in Fig. 27, and they do not necessitate any variation in the width of the building. There are horses, too, which never lie down when tied up in a stall, but will do so in a box. Where a large number of horses are to be accommodated, the "double" stable at Fig. 27 is suitable, and less costly to erect, and it is not an uncommon form of building on large farms. Objection cannot be taken from a sanitary point of view to this form of stable, as ventilation and light can be amply secured in the roof, and by the insertion of air bricks just under the wall plate in the centre of each stall, as shown in the drawings. Fig. 28 is an illustration of a stable with a feeding passage, which although desirable in many respects is too costly for general adoption. The racks are of the "low" type, at the side and on a level with the mangers, and the principal advantage gained is that the wall space in front of the horses can be supplied with windows for light and ventilation, and there is no doubt that defects of vision would be less frequent if light was more freely given in this position. Sir F. Fitzwygram, in his work on cavalry stables, was a strong advocate for windows in front of the horses, and he placed them in his designs over the mangers, the walls being made high enough for the purpose. The feeding of the horses can also proceed with greater despatch if the passage communicates, as it should do, with the food-store at the end of the building.

No stable is complete without a place of some kind for hay and chaff, either in it, above it, or adjoining it; but the plan most in vogue is the use of a loft above. This is an economical method of providing ample space for straw as well as hay, but it is often condemned because it obstructs

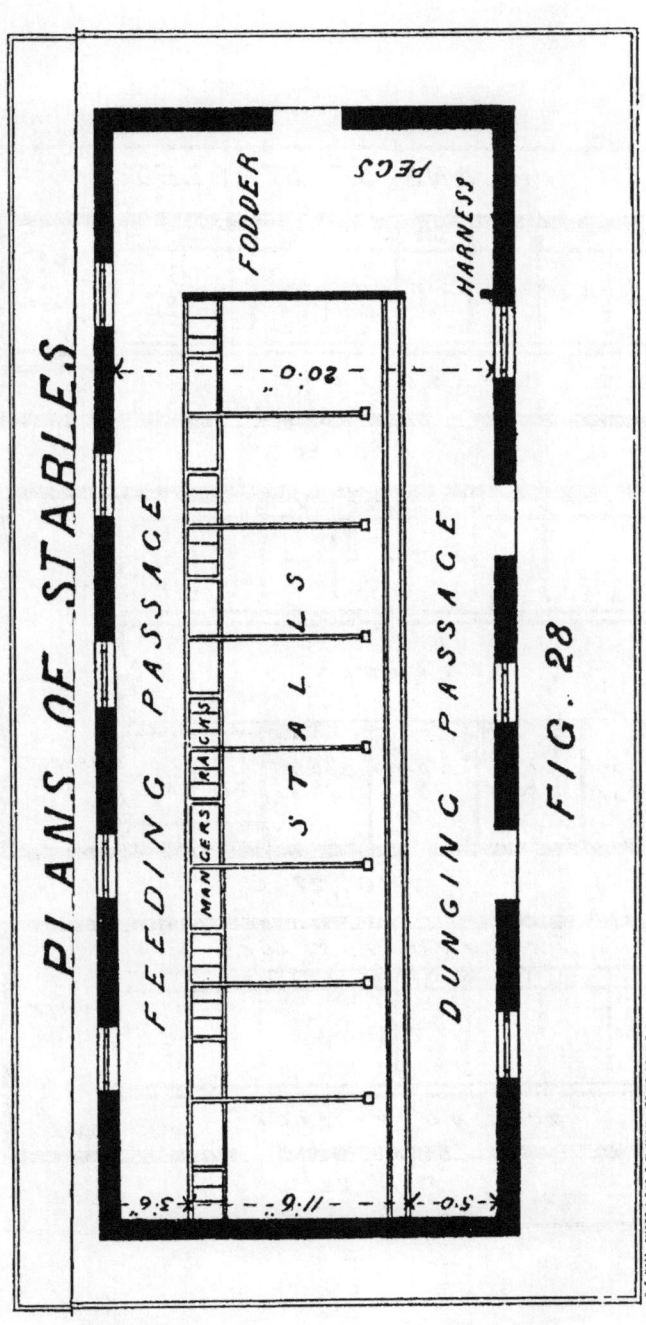

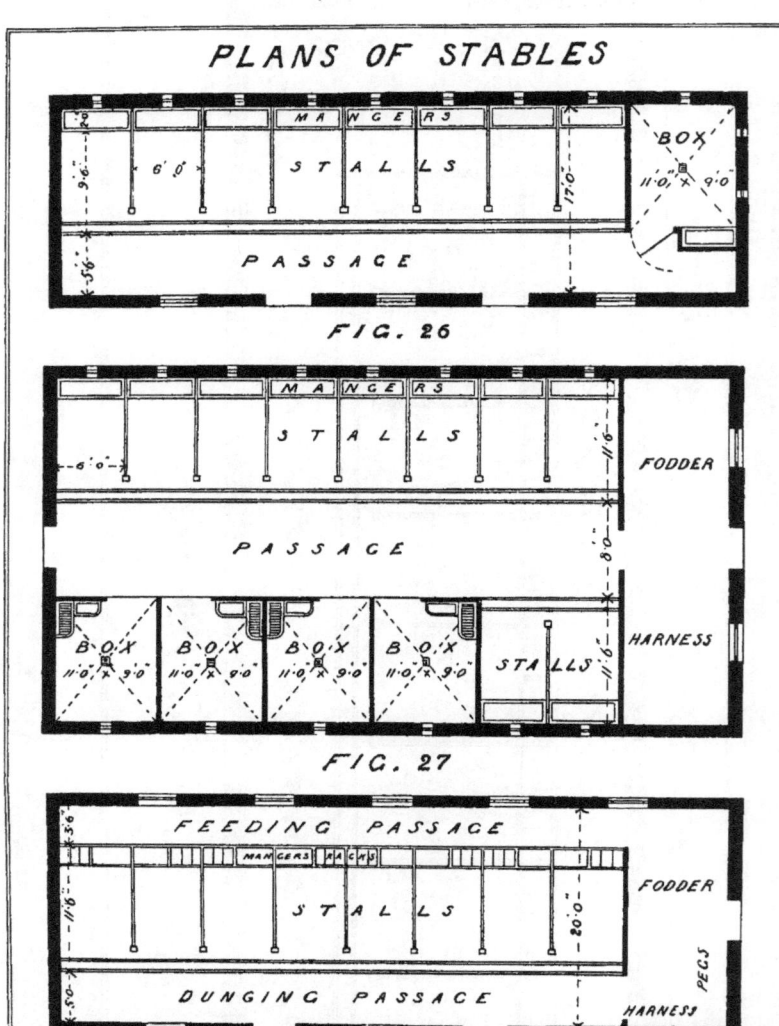

ventilation and contracts the breathing area of the stable. From the examples usually seen of old stables this objection is fully justified, but it is the result of faulty construction, which if avoided in new erections would render them free from disadvantages of the kind. The floor of the loft should be at least 9 feet above that of the stable, plenty of ventilating apertures should be put in the walls, and wooden or zinc ventilating shafts should be carried through the loft to the ridge of the roof at distances of about 12 feet apart. If this is not done, the openings in the floor through which the hay is supplied to the racks will be conductors of foul air to the hay chamber, and be very objectionable; in fact, it is better to do away with feeding from above altogether, as lazy attendants, to spare themselves trouble, habitually stuff the racks so full of hay as to give enough at one time to form several "baits," this being consequently pulled out, picked over, and half wasted. A day's supply of hay can easily be let down into a bin at the corner of the stable, and the racks filled from below, in which case the temptation to over-fill them will not be present.

On large arable farms a good deal of chaff from threshing is given to horses, which necessitates storage room; and either a capacious bin in the stable, or, what is better still, a small house adjoining, should be constructed for the purpose, and if possible it should have doors to admit a cart for the convenience of unloading. Such a place would also serve for green food in the summer-time; but of course if a straw-barn is near (as in the case in the example homesteads previously shown), the necessity for a chaff-house need not arise. Each case, however, must be governed by its attendant circumstances in this as in every other department of the homestead; but doubtless horses will be better looked after where some attempt has been made, in the arrangement of these auxiliaries, to give reasonable facilities for the feeding and attendance they require. If the stable department is so constructed as to be "self-supporting," as it may be termed, order will be promoted, roadways will not be constantly littered up by the passage of food and straw from other parts of the homestead, and carters will have no excuse for straying about the place to gossip with other workmen.

It remains, before discussing the fitting up of stables, to make a few remarks upon a place for harness. In the illustrations in this and in previous chapters, plans are given showing separate compartments as harness-rooms, but it cannot be said that they are really needed, except where a number of horses are kept, although they are very useful appendages. Where the stable is wide enough, wooden or iron pegs securely attached to the walls at the rear of the stalls are sufficient for harness in everyday use, although it will be better preserved if it is removed from the atmosphere of the stable altogether; but if there are many spare gears, or anything in the shape of best harness (and we can still see bells and rosettes in use for visits to the market town), a harness-room is really needed. Any partition dividing the same from the stable should be carried up to the loft floor, or roof, as the case may be; and, as regards the fitting up, in addition to the harness pegs, a shelf should be placed for miscellaneous articles, and a lock-up cupboard for simple remedies will be a desirable addition. Let there be abundance of light, so that the master's eye may have full play, for the men are few and far between who do not require occasionally to be reminded that the leathers and iron require oiling, and that the brasses need to be polished.

## Their Construction and Arrangement. 99

The finishing and fitting up of stables will necessitate a few remarks. As regards windows, I have seen no kind which is more suitable for farm stables than that shown at Fig. 14, and which is there recommended for general use at the homestead, the upper part being glazed, and the lower arranged for the admission of air by means of a sliding framework of wooden bars, covering at will fixed bars in the window frame. It is thoroughly suitable in every respect, as the glass, which should be rough rolled plate, is sufficiently high to lessen the risk of breakage, and the woodwork arrangement is simple and not likely to get out of order. The semi-dwelling house varieties of window occasionally met with are somewhat out of place, except in the stables of villa residences. They have only one advantage—they admit more light; but in the case of farm buildings, a few glass slates or tiles in the roof, where there is no storey above, are more effective, and not more costly.

Some remarks have already been made on ventilation. Windows in the wall at the rear, and louvres or some other form of exit at or near the ridge, will be sufficient; but where there is a chamber above, one or more air-shafts should be carried through to louvre boarding at the ridge. Failing this, two ventilating bricks might be placed to each stall, one under the manger and one above it just under the wall plate. It is more particularly where a quantity of horses are kept in one stable, that the necessity for these methods of ventilation arises, as the evidence of experts will show. While admitting that the treatment required for troop horses to keep them in health might be modified for farm horses, it is instructive to note what the Commissioners, specially appointed by the Government a few years since to report on cavalry stables, said in regard to these matters. They recommended ample ridge ventilation in every stable, openings in the slope of the roof, windows in the walls above the horses' heads, skylights in the roofs, and ventilation under the mangers.

As regards the floors of stables, to some extent what has been said upon the floors of cattle-houses will apply to these also. This is so particularly in respect of a smooth, hard, and non-absorbent surface being advantageous in saving litter, and preventing foulness of atmosphere. On many estates materials are to be found more or less suitable for paving floors, and for the sake of economy it will be well to use them where careful preparation and laying will ensure efficiency. Hard descriptions of building stone answer the purpose very well if hammered to an even face, laid on a firm foundation in sand, and grouted with cement or good mortar. Stone pebbles are not to be despised if nothing better is to be had, but the surface they give is uneven, unless they are very carefully laid. With regard to bricks, none but the hardest descriptions will stand the wear of horses' feet, such as the blue Staffordshire ware, and clinkers made for the purpose; but these will be found expensive articles if they have to be resorted to. I have, however, used good blue building bricks on edge, and found them durable for the stalls; and also the hardest burnt red local bricks on edge for the passages with success, as the wear is not so excessive there. Where straw is a scarce commodity, a little expense in obtaining a floor which will easily run off the liquids, is doubtless soon refunded in the straw saved, and for this purpose cement concrete is much recommended. For heavy cart horses, however, it is necessary to be laid of considerable thickness, but as it is difficult in country districts to get it properly repaired, we do not strongly advocate its use. The concrete should certainly be 1½ inches thick, laid on a well-prepared foundation of rubble ; and if well laid, the floor can be made particularly neat and serviceable, as grooves and channels can be formed in it in any direction for drainage.

The inclination of the surface of the floors of stalls is an important point. A slight gradient—the slighter the better for the horse—must be given for drainage ; but it is a necessary evil. We see instances sometimes where, by gross carelessness in laying the floors, the fore-legs of horses are made to stand 6 inches higher than the hind-legs, and it is no wonder that under such conditions the horses, except when feeding, are generally seen standing back as far as they can into the passage to obtain a more level footing. A fall of 1 inch in the yard for stalls with a good surface is sufficient ; but where they are more or less uneven, from the use of rough materials, something more than this will be required.

The channel or drain at the rear of the horses should always be strong and well laid. I have used with success a drain formed of blue bricks, in the manner shown in Fig. 13, as it has the advantage of sufficient width to allow of the free passage of a shovel for clearing away the manure. Various kinds of local stone will of course be often used, but careful selection and laying are needed, and of course it is scarcely possible to lay such material in the same advantageous manner as the bricks adapt themselves to in the design mentioned.

In the plans of stables which have been submitted, it will be seen that gratings are shown as indicating the presence of cesspools under, but it will be much better if the surface drains are continued to the outside of the stable and discharged on to the manure in the yards, or otherwise into cesspits connected with the drainage system. The advantages of the method were pointed out under the heading of cow-houses, therefore it will not be necessary to refer to them again.

We now come to the question of stall divisions, or travises. Sometimes these are omitted altogether, but unquestionably horses are less likely to be injured when each one stands in its own stall, which should be 6 feet in width. Where, however, the space allows not more than 5 feet for a horse, the divisions had better be omitted, as an animal cannot lie down and rise with safety for want of room. The old-fashioned method of constructing the travis is by far the most useful for farm stables, and is as follows:—A "heel" post, standing about 5 feet out of the ground, should be firmly fixed, and morticed for three rails, the other ends of which should be secured in the wall at the manger, taking care to keep the lowest one 6 inches off the ground to prevent decay from moisture. The rails should be sheeted with $1\frac{1}{4}$-inch boarding, on one side only. This is a simple, strong, and effective piece of work, and admits of a defective board being replaced with unskilled labour at any time; and most of us know that if it is a case for a joiner, the job is too often neglected until it becomes of larger extent, or some injury arises. Occasional departures from this plan are sometimes met with, smarter in appearance perhaps, but not so serviceable. The top and bottom rails are grooved, and the ends of the boards are inserted, light rails being nailed on each side about half-way up, and sometimes the boards are placed horizontally into grooved posts; but obviously, in either of these systems, it is difficult to replace a damaged board.

All the sharp edges of posts, rails, and door jambs should be chamfered off, and the brickwork jambs of all doorways should be constructed of bull-nosed or splayed bricks. Doors should be 4 feet wide in the clear, as if a horse hurts itself in going in or out it is often difficult to get it through afterwards without either hesitation or rushing through in a dangerous manner. Framed doors are of very neat appearance, but for hard farm wear, and facility of repair, $1\frac{1}{4}$-inch ledged doors, grooved and tongued, are more useful, as there are no morticings to weaken them. Doors which open into yards occupied by stock should be hung in halves, as when air and light are required the upper portion can remain open, while the latter can be closed to prevent the entry of animals into the stable.

There are many varieties of mangers, the cheapest perhaps being made of $1\frac{1}{2}$-inch planking, with a 4 by 3 oak "chin" rail, properly bevelled, and fixed on the top of the front plank. It should be properly supported, midway between the travises, with short oak posts, which also serve for affixing the rings for fastening up the horses. This class of manger is most generally in use, being efficient and durable; but if anything smarter or cleaner in its appearance and use is required, there are of course many kinds made of brickwork, one of which, for cows, shown at Fig. 16 on page 65, is often used in stables. Its chief feature is the manger brick for the front, which gives the necessary stability, the back and bottom being formed with smooth quarries, cement or otherwise, according to inclination. A base of brickwork is of course necessary to support the structure; this should be solid, but an aperture should be made, and an arch turned over it, to form a place for turning back the unsoiled litter when the stall is cleaned out. The "roll" on the top of the manger brick in the illustration referred to prevents horses turning their food out.

The question of racks for stables has been the source of

some controversy. Some persons prefer, instead of the usual method of placing them above the manger on a line with the horses' heads, to fix low ones on a level with the manger, such as that indicated at Fig. 28, where it is shown in connection with a feeding passage; but it does equally well placed against the stable wall without the passage. On the whole, and from experience, I should say the low rack is preferable. It is more in accordance with the natural position of the horse when grazing; seeds and dust are not liable to drop into the horse's eyes; it is easily supplied with fodder; and is not open to the objections referred to in a previous chapter which attend the filling of racks from the lofts above. In the matter of construction it may be very simple. Half the width of the stall is occupied by it, and the other half by the manger; and if the wooden "chin" rail which has been referred to is used for the manger, it is continued so as to form the top rail of the rack, the staves being fixed perpendicularly. The bottom may be of brickwork or wood, 6 inches from the floor, and sloped upwards to prevent the accumulation of seeds, and a bar can be placed across the top to prevent the hay being turned out by the horse.

Of iron racks and mangers little need be said, as the numerous advertisements of the makers describe them fully. Their expense is probably a drawback to their more general use, and as usually made, the racks are not sufficiently capacious for holding hay for farm horses, and seem only adapted for the more moderate feeds of carriage horses; and, with few exceptions, the same may be said as regards the mangers.

The finishing and fitting up of the interior of stables, as with all other farm buildings, should be simple, and adapted as much as possible for easy repair by ordinary village workmen, so that when the dilapidation stage is reached there may be no excuse for delay and letting matters go from bad to worse. Careless tenants are apt to say, when remonstrated with, "Well, we didn't know where to get a man that *could* do the job!"

## CHAPTER X.

### PIGGERIES.

IT seems so natural to hear pigs abused for their dirty ways, that it is hard to conceive that they are in some respects much more cleanly in their habits when in confinement than other farm stock. They are more attached to warmth and comfort than any other animal under the farmer's charge, and undoubtedly they play a very important part in the farming economy of the homestead, although their aid as "rent-payers" has been neglected in the past on many occupations. Owing doubtless to the low price, often prevailing, of grain, and the want of a medium for its consumption, this neglect is being remedied to a considerable extent. If the movements of pigs are noted when in confinement, the cleanly habits and ideas of comfort which we refer to will soon become apparent. They invariably use one corner for their exuviæ, and reserve a place, which is kept as clean as possible, to lie down on; and it is very interesting to watch them carrying clean straw in their mouths to make their beds as dry and comfortable as they can. It is fortunate perhaps that they can accommodate themselves—at some loss to their owners, however—to the many forms of neglect to which they are often subjected, but there can be scarcely any doubt that no animals sooner repay the cost of additional comfort supplied, or liberal treatment bestowed upon them.

## Their Construction and Arrangement. 107

They are, unlike most domesticated animals, scantily provided by nature with hair, consequently shelter and warmth are necessary in a greater degree.

So much may be said for the animals and their habits before discussing plans for their habitation. It appears to me that the almost invariable method of providing small sties, each with its small yard, is not always a desirable one to follow. It may at least be often departed from with advantage. The typical sty has to be crept into when it requires cleaning out, owing to its small doorway, and the pigs when wanted for inspection generally run inside of it. The arrangement, moreover, is objectionable, because such a form of building is utterly unsuited for any other animals; and on a farm, or at a cottage even, every building should if possible be adapted for a variety of uses.

In order to obtain a building which is of general use, it will be necessary to resort to the "box" form of sty, as shown in the homestead designs, Figs. 1 to 7. It will scarcely be necessary to give any illustrations for so simple a structure beyond the ideas conveyed in these designs. If a box or a series of boxes, according to requirements, are built with an area 9 ft. by 9 ft., or 10 ft. by 8 ft., they would each be suitable for a sow and pigs for a litter of small stores, or for four fattening pigs; and when not in use for pigs, they would do for calves, young stock, or even fattening stock, or for sheep; or they might be used as toolhouses or stores. Some pigs of course require a run out for exercise, but all do not. Those put up for fattening will be better if confined to the pens entirely, where they will be warmer than in the ordinary sty. Breeding sows, and young growing animals to be fed for bacon, must of course have a run out, either in a small yard for each sty, or if the boxes opened into a grass paddock, they could be let out as desired; but if there is no such convenience, a fair-sized yard may be fenced in for a common run for the whole, either for their sole use, or an adjoining cattle-yard may be availed of, as when the cattle are at pasture in the day the pigs can be let out, and shut up again when they return at night. This system has been tested on various sized farms, and has been approved of by the occupiers; while as regards the landlord, it usually results in a saving of money as compared with the old method of building sties. Cottagers even prefer the boxes, as they do not always have a pig; and where none are kept, they are in possession of a useful little store, or workshop, which relieves the limited space in the cottages of many odds and ends, which can be kept elsewhere when the elsewhere is forthcoming.

As regards construction, we have already recommended an area of about 80 ft. for each box, and the walls should be about 6 ft. high. In the front a space, say 1 ft. 6 in. to 2 ft., must be left open under the eaves for sun and air, but in cold weather this aperture might be closed with a shutter, or, better still, the space might be fitted up with fixed bars and a slide, on the "hit and miss" principle shown at the window design, Fig. 14.

The "rooting-up" habits which pigs no doubt have inherited from their progenitors, who foraged for themselves in bygone times in the immense forest tracts which then abounded, must be counteracted by sound work and the use of the strongest materials, otherwise continual repairs will be needed. A floor of hard building brick, laid in mortar or in sand and well grouted, is strong, and adapted for good surface drainage such as is required to run off the large quantity of liquid voided by these animals. If cesspits with iron gratings are placed in each pen, the floor should be well dished to them; but if the drainage is taken

## Their Construction and Arrangement.

on the surface to the outside, and run into the yard to enrich the manure thrown out from the other animals, it will be better. If, however, it is necessary to carry it away by a drain, let it be conducted by a surface channel if possible to one cesspit outside the boxes, as the less of these there are about a homestead the better it is. In boxes which are used for breeding sows some provision is needed to prevent them lying close up to the walls and crushing the young ones. This is easily prevented, by fixing a 2-in. plank, about 6 in. wide, all round the walls 8 in. from the floor.

In most of the piggeries shown in the example homesteads a feeding passage is given, and where many pigs are kept it is a desirable convenience; but in Figs. 6 and 7, small doors are shown in the outer walls through which the food is put from a pathway outside. This may be carried out also by building in the walls earthenware spouts, made for the purpose, and these are stronger, the only disadvantage being that the trough is not accessible from the outside. There is an excellent feeding trough which can be introduced, with a feeding passage, whereby hungry animals can be kept back while the food is being put in. This is made of iron, but can easily also be constructed of wood, and consists of a strong shutter suspended from a rail, to hang exactly over the centre of the trough. When the food is being put in, the shutter is pushed inwards, and a bolt dropped, which throws the whole of the trough in the passage; and by swinging the shutter back and bolting it to the other side of the trough, the whole of the trough is thus at the service of the pigs. Of course everything must be strong for an arrangement of this kind, and where wood is used it should be oak, and protected by iron hooping or sheet iron.

Sparred flooring, such as that previously described for calf-houses (see Fig. 19), is sometimes used for pigs, to economise straw. The animals do not look so comfortable as when on litter, and there is no advantage beyond the saving of straw when it is scarce or dear; but, on the other hand, there may be a disadvantage in winter, as the sties will not be so warm where the system is adopted, and fattening will be retarded in consequence.

A food-house is a very serviceable addition to a piggery, and at the example homesteads, Figs. 1 to 5, it is shown in connection therewith. If fitted up properly, it should contain a large iron furnace pan for cooking food, a cistern for wash below ground, and space should be given for troughs for meal and for mixing up food, the latter being tenant's fixtures. The underground cistern will be found particularly useful if the liquids from the scullery and dairy can be discharged through pipes into it by gravitation, as this not only saves labour, but, given such facilities, servants are not likely to waste these products by throwing them down the nearest drain to save trouble. Moreover, when the cistern is placed below ground and against an outer wall, the wash can be tipped up from a tub on wheels directly into it, provided the pipe arrangement from the house is not practicable. The furnace pan, or boiler, should always adjoin the cistern, so that the wash can be easily laded into it. When roots are boiled it is better to use "wash" instead of water, if it is at hand, as they already contain some 90 per cent. of water; and the food trough should be close to the boiler, so that the cooked materials can be cast into it direct. Where the piggery is extensive it will be desirable to allow for the admission of carts to be unloaded direct into the store; or where this is not done, labour can be saved by having a small door in the outer wall, above the boiler through which roots or potatoes can be passed into it. This door will also assist the escape of steam, but some form of ridge ventilation will be needed as well.

A food-house of suitable dimensions, fitted up with due regard to these principles, will be a serviceable addition to any homestead at which a number of pigs are kept. As to the merits of cooking food, it is almost impossible to feed a lot of pigs suitably, and without waste, unless the boiler is sometimes resorted to. Of course it will not answer to light a fire for cooking every day for two or three animals, but an occasional warm meal in winter-time assists the fattening process, and provides a beneficial change of diet. Young pigs when weaned undoubtedly thrive better on cooked food.

It may also be pointed out that on stock-rearing farms the pigs' food-house is a convenient place for erecting a small open fireplace (one flue being sufficient for this and the boiler) at which calves' food can be heated, mashes made, and men made comfortable when sitting up on cold nights in attendance upon cows calving or ewes in the lambing season.

## CHAPTER XI.

### CART-SHEDDING AND MISCELLANEOUS BUILDINGS.

THE remarks upon this part of the homestead do not require to be of much length, owing to the simple construction of the buildings. Some of them will not be necessary at all, except in the case of large occupations or at model or home farms; but they are all shown at one or more of the example homesteads, and the subject will not be complete without some slight reference to them, as there are errors to be avoided and points to be mentioned deserving of consideration.

### CART-SHEDDING.

The amount of shedding needed for carts, waggons, and implements has of late years been more extended, owing to the greater variety of articles brought into use. It will not be necessary to enumerate these, but it will be evident that arable farms of a given acreage will require more storage space for implements than pastoral farms of the same extent. Situation is the first point for attention, and the nearer the stable the storage can be placed, consistently with other circumstances, the better it will be, as there is a close working affinity in these parts. Secondly, as regards dimensions, the openings should not be less than 9 ft. in the clear, with one about 10 ft. for large

## Their Construction and Arrangement. 113

drills and horse rakes, which sometimes require it. To properly protect a waggon, 20 ft. in depth is necessary, and two carts can be housed in the same space, but implements can of course be conveniently placed in narrower buildings. Aspect should be studied, and the entry of sun and rain avoided as much as possible, a north-eastern exposure being the best. For a similar reason the eaves should not be too high, not more than 7 ft. 6 in. or 8 ft. from the ground. The back wall of cart or implement shedding forms an excellent boundary and shelter for a stockyard, and a simple lean to roof against any building offering facilities for the same, will provide an economical store for such small articles as plough, harrows, &c., and the eaves may be nearer the ground than those of a cart-shed. For the better preservation of expensive implements, like drills, it is advisable to have one opening in a line of shedding, or elsewhere, closed with a pair of doors, which a tenant can put a lock upon if he chooses. The buildings here referred to are of course shown in position in the plans of homesteads, Figs. 1 to 7, in the earlier chapters.

The best place for storing tools will be in close connection with the cart-shedding, as ropes, forks, rakes, and the like, are given out to or brought back by the carters for safe keeping,—or perhaps it would be more correct to say that under orderly management this is the case. Every article ought to be in its place in the tool-house, and if this is placed in the position here recommended, everything will be at hand when wanted, and there will be one excuse less for the teams hanging back when they ought to be on their way to work. In addition to the usual pegs for hanging the tools up, a shelf should be run along one side for very small articles.

## CARPENTER'S AND BLACKSMITH'S SHOPS.

It is only on extensive farms, where the repairs to the implements and premises, and the shoeing, are sufficient for the employment of a carpenter or wheelwright, and a blacksmith, for at least a day a week, that these appendages to the homestead are needed; and sometimes tenants of farms will provide them at their own cost, where village shops of the kind are distant, rather than incur the inevitable loss of time of men and horses travelling to and from such places. Of the two, perhaps the blacksmith's shop is the more needed, on account of shoeing operations being so frequent where there are a number of horses; but the introduction of both shops would yield a saving of the tradesmen's profits on the iron and timber used, and as regards the latter no doubts would then arise as to the quality used.

At Figs. 1 and 3 are shown carpenter's and blacksmith's shops; in convenient situations attached to the ranges of cart-shedding, where they are close to the articles to be repaired, and in each design an adjoining bay of the cart-shed is shown as having a boarded partition for forming it into a place for tying horses up while being shod, the bay at other times being used for carts or implements.

The fitting up of a carpenter's shop will be a small matter either for landlord or tenant, and it must be presumed that frequently both these conveniences will fall to the latter to provide. One or two shelves should be fixed up, also a few drawers or lockers for nails or screws. The work bench should be a portable one, as it may be of occasional use elsewhere.

In a blacksmith's shop should be built the usual hearth, with an iron curb about one foot wide placed round it.

The lower part of the flue will require a sheet-iron hood attached to it, the bottom of which should be about two feet from the hearth. This plan is preferable to carrying the flue up from the hearth itself, as is sometimes done, because of the increased space left for working operations. A strong working bench should be placed near the window, and the bellows, water trough, anvil, and vice will all be tenant's fixtures. Plenty of light is necessary where all work goes on, and the doors of both shops should be hung in halves.

### SICK BOXES AND SLAUGHTER-HOUSES.

These are decided extras in the way of ordinary farm accommodation, but as they are sometimes met with, the subject will not be complete without a short reference to them.

On large farms carrying a number of valuable animals it is sometimes thought prudent to put up buildings of this kind. A sick box, placed out of the reach of healthy animals, will be of service for contagious ailments, as well as for the proper treatment of other casual cases; and it seems desirable to place it in close connection with a slaughter-house, as when an animal is not likely to be brought round by treatment, and is in a condition to yield wholesome food if properly slaughtered and dressed, a suitable place for this will therefore be close at hand. The absence of means and appliances for thus making the best of animals suddenly attacked or injured beyond recovery often leads to considerable losses; and it will be evident, that although it is a comparatively easy matter to slay a heavy beast, its value will be very little unless it is hung up and properly dressed, hence the necessity of some suitable place, with winding apparatus and a boiler for heating water.

A sick box or "infirmary," and a slaughter-house, are shown and described in connection with Fig. 1 of the example homesteads in one of the early chapters, and also at Fig. 3. Complete isolation of the former is not there given, although it is more desirable that it should be entirely disconnected from the homestead.

### MANURE TANKS AND DRAINAGE.

Observation in the matter of liquid manure tanks and drainage has convinced me that much money is frequently spent upon them with useless or bad effect. The following extract from the paper (referred to in preceding chapters) read by me at the Surveyors' Institution will show the result of this experience :—" A few words on the subject of drainage and liquid manure tanks must not be omitted, as much money is frequently spent upon these works with useless or bad effect. As a general rule tenants will not use these tanks, but why they neglect to do so I cannot understand. They will doubtless tell you that they value a cup of strong tea more than the leaves left in the teapot, and will make a very sensible use of it; but they fail to recognise the value of the strong decoction washed out of the manure, which they may have purchased cake mainly to enrich. On one estate, I knew of eight or nine expensively constructed large tanks, properly fed with a system of drainage and supplied with lead pumps, which remained unused for years; therefore I would strongly recommend that money should not be wasted in constructing them, unless there be a good probability of their intelligent use. But the question may then be asked, Are we deliberately to turn this stream of fertilising matter into the nearest ditch? My reply would be, Make as little as possible of it; properly trough all eaves; divert all surface water on roadways from entering the yards; use corrugated iron instead of tiles or slates for the usual shedding of open yards, so as to cover in a greater area at the same expense; and apply the money which would be expended in tanks, pumps, and drainage, to covering in a still larger proportion, remembering that if a ton of manure occupy two square yards of surface,—which it will do if eighteen inches thick,—that a ton and a half of rain-water descends upon it in a year according to a rainfall of thirty-six inches, which is the average in some districts. A very small tank will then suffice for the drainage from the stalls, but even this need not be collected if litter be plentiful, as it might be discharged on the surface of the yards; but I should not recommend this being done if these be not covered, as they would be rendered still more uncomfortable for stock.

"With regard to drainage, if this is not carried out in the simplest and best manner, stoppages will be the result, as the cleaning out of cesspools is persistently neglected by farm servants. I remember a case, at an extensive homestead, where it cost £40 to clean out and rearrange a complicated and ineffective system for a new tenant. The course of all drains should be perfectly straight, and run from cesspool to cesspool, as these will form places of observation for determining the exact locality of any stoppage without disturbing unnecessary ground, and give facility for inserting a piece of fence wire from one to another for its displacement. Avoid all curves where a deviation from a direct course is imperative, by laying the pipes in two straight lines, and constructing a brick joint at the point where they meet, carrying it up to the surface for the same uses; and let all pipes be six inches in diameter, taking care to use socketed ones when passing near the source of any supply of water for domestic purposes."

Notwithstanding the foregoing unfavourable experience in regard to manure tanks, others may take a more sanguine view of their proper use if provided. An economical method of construction is as follows :—On a concrete foundation build up the walls in brick with a 9-in. course of "headers" to every four courses of stretchers, that is $4\frac{1}{2}$-in. work only, and the walls thus built will be strong enough if not more than 8 ft. high. If the tank exceeds 8 ft. long, it should have a cross wall in the centre (turned on an arch to save space) for support against the pressure of the soil at the sides. The walls should of course have proper footings, and the bottom be laid with bricks on the concrete; or if more strength is required, an inverted arch should be built of $4\frac{1}{2}$-in. work, and a similar arch, or a 9-in. one, should be turned over the top, with manhole or cover. The inside surface should be rendered with two coats of cement, with the usual proportion of two parts sand, to make watertight, and an overflow drain inserted.

The best kind of pump for a thick liquid like manure is the "Simplex" pump, now pretty well known, as it is cheap, and not so likely to get out of order as the ordinary lead or iron pump; in fact it cannot be beaten for farm purposes.

Manure tanks may be dispensed with, without incurring a waste of the fertilising liquid, by discharging the mouth of the collecting drain on to the surface of an adjoining pasture where the levels permit, and distributing the matter on the surface by means of channels cut out of the turf, which is a simple method of irrigation. In this case the volume discharged should be diluted, and increased as much as possible by collecting roofing and other surface water. Where the levels do not permit of following out this plan, sometimes the drain is discharged into a pit into which any rubbish may be cast to absorb its contents. This is removed at intervals, and forms a valuable top-dressing for pastures. Either of these methods entails but little outlay, and supplies the means of preventing waste.

### WATER SUPPLY.

An unfailing pond of water, if kept free from pollution by drainage from the yards, is a great boon to any homestead, and in nine cases out of ten it is sufficient, and satisfies the tenants. Unfortunately, however, there are situations where it is impossible to obtain a supply of this kind, and much difficulty and expenditure of money have to be encountered before the deficiency is remedied. This is the case more particularly in light land districts, where ponds, it is true, exist, but they fail in summer when most needed. If a pond fails in this manner occasionally, a tenant is expected to put up with such temporary inconvenience if the well for domestic purposes is available, notwithstanding the labour which may be involved in carrying water to the stock, where the well is unfavourably situated for pumping into a trough to which the stock should have access. But it is where a natural supply (as it may be termed) of this kind is not obtainable, at a reasonable outlay, that artificial means have to be resorted to.

Of late, where ponds and pumps have proved troublesome and unreliable, there has been a tendency to avoid expenditure upon them, if an alternative scheme of supply presents itself; therefore, before incurring expenditure in a matter upon which there might be a doubt as to permanent efficiency, it will be well to get information as to the surroundings. If a spring can be found on higher ground within a reasonable distance, the difficulty will be solved in the most favourable way; but if not, a stream of a lower level, if existing, may be utilised by means of a ram or turbine, or water-wheel working a force pump; and, failing this, there will be no other resource than to collect and store rain-water in tanks. The whole subject is an interesting one, but to enter upon full details would be much beyond the scope of this work. Since the passing of the Public Health Acts in 1875, the question of a pure water supply has been brought into prominence, and the County Councils appear, so far, ready to turn their attention to any shortcomings existing in rural districts. A sanitary expert, Dr James Ellis, in a valuable little book, "A Working Guide and Note Book on important Public Health Subjects," states that "a very large number of epidemics of typhoid fever have been traced to fouled water supplied to the dairy." We may as well, therefore, take the hints which this activity shows, and, when any defects in water supply present themselves for a remedy, try to obtain a supply which will be beyond suspicion as regards its purity. Nothing is so likely to yield this as the tapping of a spring in the fields, if such exists, and bringing down the water by gravitation. It will supply the house as well as the homestead, and possibly other houses and cottages can be included in the scheme.

Many a useful spring or supply of water has been obliterated by an ordinary land drain, and it is surprising to the uninitiated how small a stream, a mere "trickle" in fact, will suffice to supply even a moderate-sized village with water if it is constantly running. I have in my mind many supplies of this kind, which have been successful, at

## Their Construction and Arrangement. 121

a most moderate cost, both on a small as well as a large scale, but as we are dealing only with farm supplies I must confine my remarks thereto.  If the spring is a very weak one, but not unless it is so, a storage tank large enough to accumulate the supply is necessary, and a galvanised iron pipe of 1 in. diameter, costing about 9d. a yard, is sufficient to conduct the water to any extensive homestead.  A quarter of a mile of this, together with the laying, would cost only about £22, and the repairs or after-cost involved would, as regards bringing it to the homestead, be a mere trifle.

A ram or turbine, where it was practicable to fix one, would be a more expensive affair, and should therefore only be employed as a last resource, when every other method failed, unless the distance from the same to the homestead was a very moderate one entailing a small outlay in pipes.

Hydraulic rams are machines which are rendered self-acting by means of a delivery pipe from a lake, stream, or canal, with a fall of not less than 8 ft.  This would raise the water to a height of about 80 ft. by automatically closing a valve leading to the waste-pipe in the ram, and lifting up a valve at the entrance of an air chamber, the result being a compression of air which, as the operation repeats itself, forces a portion of the water up the rising main.  Some 800 to 1,000 gallons of water daily may be thus raised with a 2-in. supply pipe and 1-in. rising main; and of course more powerful rams which can command a better supply of water and greater fall are capable of raising a supply of many thousand gallons daily.  The water from a spring on a hill-side is sometimes collected in an open reservoir to feed a ram below for a certain number of hours daily, which raises the water to a storage tank of the necessary height to supply a house and buildings by gravitation.  An arrangement of this kind has been in satisfactory use for many years in my own village, but as not above 1 gallon in 8 of water entering rams is lifted to its destination, periods of drought will sometimes lessen the supply inconveniently. The new self-regulating windmills are coming much in favour for raising water where the situation is favourable for obtaining sufficient wind, as to which an expert should be consulted. Their utility over rams is that they waste no water, but to cover periods of calm weather, considerable storage capacity is needed.

Probably, as an alternative to the supply by gravitation, a system of storage tanks supplied from the roofing water will be found in most cases to be the best. If not previously spouted, the advantage of doing so to the buildings, roadways, and manure at a homestead, is alone worth the expense of this part of the work. As regards the description of tank best suited for the purpose, a brick and cement one, such as was described for liquid manure, will be the cheapest, if required underground. If of a size to hold several thousand gallons, they can be built, to include excavation and fitting up with an iron pump, at the rate of about 2d. per gallon, while iron tanks would cost about double the amount. Where, however, there are a number of high or two-storey buildings, and it is desired that pumping should be dispensed with, it will be a good plan to place one or more iron tanks on the floor of the upper storey, from which water can be directed to the cattle troughs, the engine boiler, or other requisite supplies.

In connection with these artificial systems of water supply—that is, those involving the convenience of a storage at a level permitting gravitation to such parts of the homestead as need it—there will arise the question of its distribution for use. There appears to be a general opinion that it is better to have a constant supply of water in troughs in the yards, as it is beneficial to the stock, and the same may be said as regards stalls and boxes; but owing to the expense attending the latter there are very few tenant farmers who will aspire to such a convenience. As regards the supply for the yards, however, the cost being so reasonable, no objection need arise. The main point to be observed is, to lay the supply pipe with as few vertical bends as possible, for although water is supposed to find its level through the pipes, this may go on so tardily as to be almost a failure where the fall from the original source is slight. In selecting a position for a trough, let it be if possible just outside one of the buildings, in order that a "supply box" containing the ball valve may be placed inside, where it will be free from the effects of frost and other injury. This is on the supposition that the system is to be self-feeding, which is much better than a supply from a tap. Where a trough cannot be placed in such a position, it should have a small compartment at one end of it to contain the ball valve, the lid of which can be fastened with a padlock; and usually one trough can be made to serve either two yards, by placing it in the fence between them, or for one yard and for the horses, if it is fixed in the division between the yard and a roadway to which the horses can have access. One-inch galvanised iron tubes costing about 1s. per yard are sufficient for ordinary mains, and ¾ in. at about 9d. per yard will do for branch pipes about a homestead.

As regards a self-feeding supply for the manger of each beast in a range of stalls and boxes, it is certain to be a work of a costly nature, but it is sometimes done. If existing mangers without the necessary fittings have to be so supplied, they may require to be almost entirely reconstructed; but a system of supply which is not self-feeding can be introduced with much less expense, by providing a standpipe at some convenient point and attaching to it a length of hose to distribute the water to each manger, in which can be placed a small iron trough held in position by some simple contrivance, or one such box may be made to serve for two beasts. Cattle-boxes, where the mangers require heightening as the manure accumulates, can be admirably supplied with water on this plan, and cow-house floors can be washed down.

There will of course be other parts of large homesteads which require to participate in the supply of water where a good overhead cistern or cisterns exist, such as the steam-engine, the food-stores, the boiling-house attached to the piggery, and sometimes a milk-cooler. The latter is often the source of much waste of water, therefore I should recommend that after it has passed from the cooler (unless it can be utilised in some other way) it should be run into a tank to be pumped up again for future use.

In estimating the size of store tanks required for a homestead where rainfall only is to supply them, the area of buildings from which the water is collected should be ascertained, also the average rainfall of the district, which will vary from 30 to 36 in. or more, calculating $6\frac{1}{4}$ gallons to equal a cubic foot. Horses and cattle require about 10 gallons per head per diem, but it must not be forgotten that the water-cart is often required to be at work in the summer for sheep.

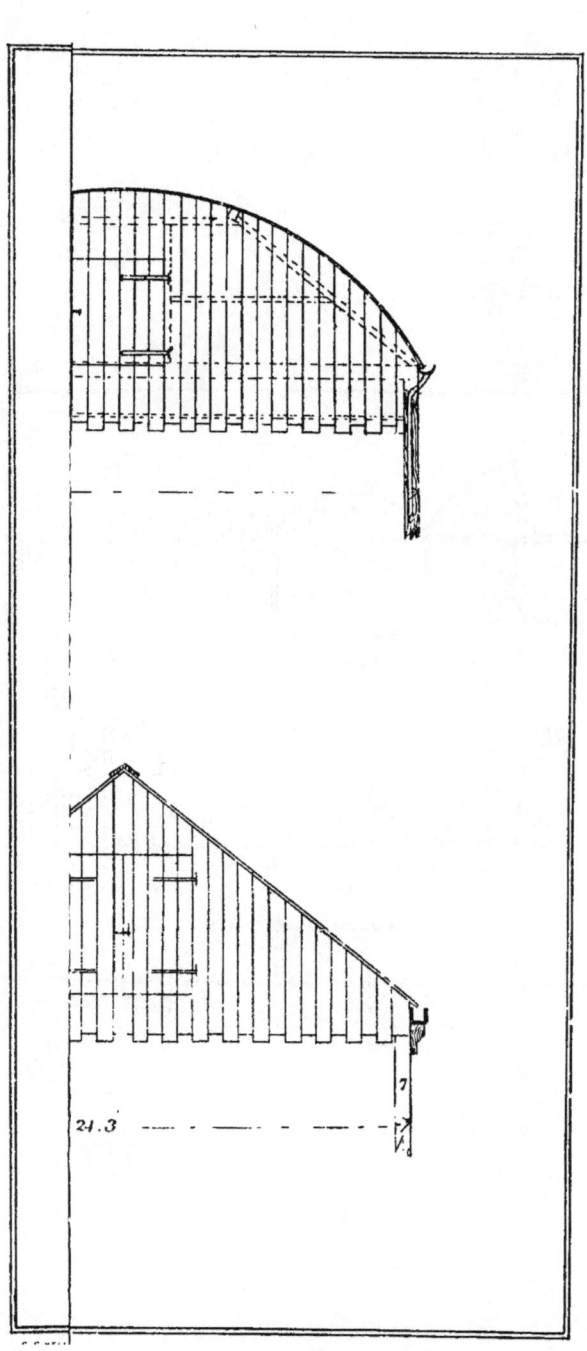

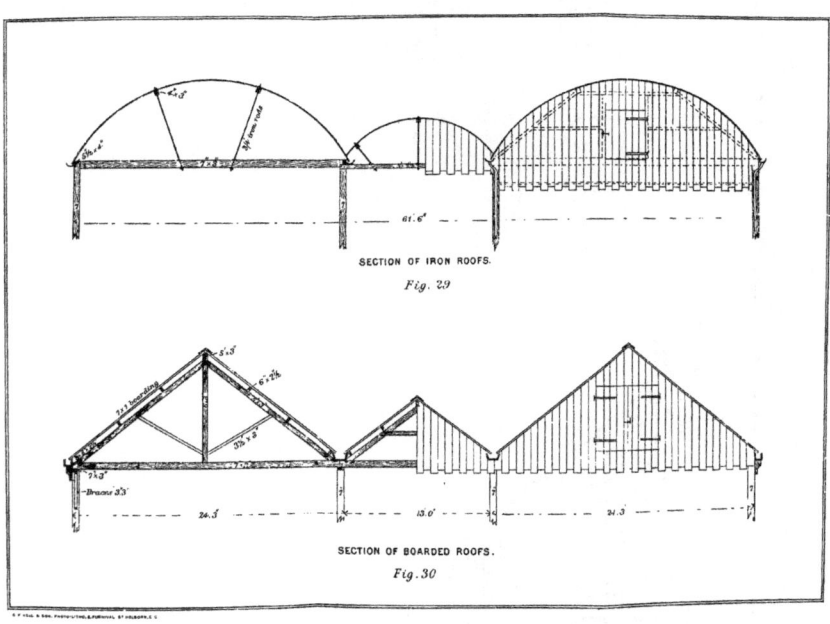

SECTION OF IRON ROOFS.

*Fig. 29*

SECTION OF BOARDED ROOFS.

*Fig. 30*

C F KELL & SON, PHOTO-LITHO, 8 FURNIVAL ST HOLBORN, E.C.

## CHAPTER XII.

### DUTCH BARN AND OTHER ROOFING.

THE increasing popularity of Dutch barns and the necessity of providing cheap and durable roofing for them, as well as for sheds for cattle and other farm purposes, necessitates a more detailed examination of the roofing question than that given in the chapter on covered yards.

It will not be necessary to dwell upon the advantages, which are so well known, of providing buildings which will preserve crops, stock, and implements from injury; but it may be borne in mind that the difficulty, which appears to be increasing in some districts, of obtaining sufficient labour, has increased the demand for Dutch barns to save the time taken up in thatching stacks.

Occasionally a controversy has arisen as to the comparative cost and merits of iron and wood roofs, and I will endeavour to throw some light upon the subject by a reference to the two sectional illustrations here given which will be more serviceable for the purpose than the elevations and "views" which are so numerous in the trade lists. At Fig. 29 is shown, in section, the curved corrugated iron roofs of two Dutch barns recently erected, each 50 ft. long by 24 ft. 3 in. wide, with a covered driving way between them 13 ft. wide, the whole covering an area (including eaves beyond the posts) of 62 ft. 6 in. by 50 ft., or 348 yards superficial; and the section at Fig. 30 is given to show wooden roofs of the same dimensions for purposes of comparison.

As regards these examples it should be understood that the idea at first was to erect a single iron roof of double the length; but it was afterwards decided to put them, as shown, in 50 ft. lengths, with the covered driving way (which is convenient for unloading and threshing in wet weather), as the advantage could be cheaply purchased.

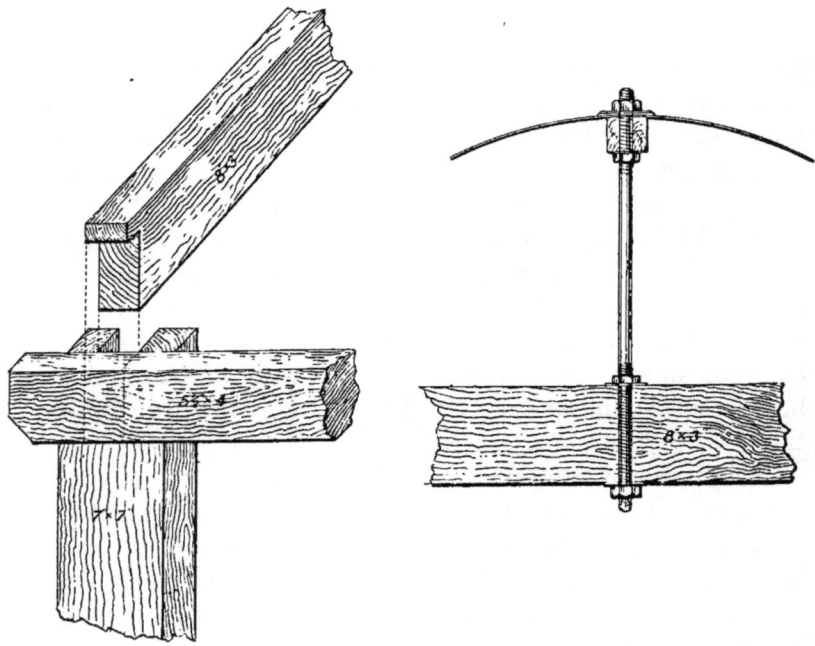

FIG. 31.

Two extra posts only were wanted, and the structure being in a block is stronger and gives greater resistance to storms than a long single roof. The posts, which are 7 in. by 7 in. and creosoted, are 12 ft. 6 in. apart, support plates 5½ in. by 4 in., and tie beams 7 in. by 3 in. There are two light wood purlins 4 in. by 3 in. running the length of the main roofs, to which the iron roofing is screwed, and at each tie beam two queen rods are inserted and bolted through on the outside of the roof, by this means trussing and making the roof rigid.

This combination of light timbers with iron rods, which is more clearly shown in detail at Fig. 31, is not the method of construction in common use; but after erecting many iron roofs, I have adopted the principle as being easily carried out by ordinary estate carpenters, and because the roofs keep their true shape to a greater degree than where iron tie rods are used, as the latter are apt to droop and carry the curved roofing down with them, particularly when farmers, as they sometimes do, weight them with ladders and other things they want to store away.

The roofs are boarded down at the ends, which gives them a serviceable and neat appearance, and the eaves are troughed. A novel feature in connection with the fixing of the driving way roof, is the discharge of its eaves on to the main roofs, so that the eaves troughing fixed on these roofs acts as an economical substitute for that expensive article, a gutter, which would otherwise be required. The eaves troughing has the advantage also of being easily accessible from the inside in case of a stoppage.

The actual cost of this barn is as follows :—

### MATERIALS.

| | £ | s. | d. |
|---|---|---|---|
| Corrugated iron roofing, 22 gauge - | 40 | 0 | 0 |
| 20 creosoted posts, 150 ft. cube at 3s. | 22 | 10 | 0 |
| Roof timber and boards - - - | 18 | 15 | 0 |
| Bolts, rods, nails, &c. - - - | 9 | 14 | 0 |
| Eaves, gutter, down-pipes, &c. - - | 4 | 19 | 0 |

### LABOUR.

| | £ | s. | d. |
|---|---|---|---|
| Carpenter's labour erecting - - | 10 | 12 | 0 |
| Labourer's     „          „       - - | 8 | 5 | 0 |
| Total | £114 | 15 | 0 |

This sum represents for the 348 yards of ground covered, a sum of 6s. 7d. per yard as near as may be. A reference to the expenditure on similar roofs erected gives corresponding results, the chief variations being in the slight changes in the cost of iron, and in respect of the posts, which, it will be seen, being creosoted deal, are an expensive item, costing 22s. 6d. each. Occasionally good larch grown on the estate has been used, and on one occasion I was enabled to buy some creosoted telegraph poles (which had been replaced with larger ones by the Post Office department) at a low price, a considerable saving being effected in each of these cases. A slightly cheaper form of roof, of flat corrugated iron on timber, can, however, be constructed, of which more later.

The wooden roofs shown at Fig. 30 cover the same area as the foregoing, but the whole erection is of creosoted wood, on the principle advocated by Mr Moscrop (and others) and explained by him in an article in the *Journal of the Royal Agricultural Society* (Vol. I., Part 3, 3rd series, 1890). I am not able, as in the case of the iron roof, to refer to it as an erection of my own; but the details of construction are taken from a roof of the kind recently erected and inspected, and I have obtained an estimate from a leading firm for the creosoted timber required, and the labour has been carefully priced by an experienced clerk of works.

The posts and tie beams are the same as those for the iron roof, but there are light king-post trusses supporting two light purlins on each side. The particular feature, however, for this class of roof is the covering with 1-in. creosoted deal boards, nailed from eaves to ridge, ¼ in. apart, to the purlins, but kept from actual contact with these by means of the heads of galvanised nails nailed into them. This ensures a space between the purlins and the boards where air will circulate and prevent the accumulation of moisture; and each board has two slight grooves, about half an inch from the edge, which form channels for intercepting driven rain (which would otherwise find its way to the apertures between the boards) and conducting the water to the eaves. The gutters are formed of inch boards pitched on the insides. The description of these roofs will, however, be materially assisted by a reference to the following brief specification:—

SPECIFICATION FOR WOOD ROOFS SHOWN AT FIG. 30.

The whole of the timber to be sound red deal, properly creosoted.

The posts, 7 by 7 in., to be well rammed 4 ft. deep in ground. Tenon the same for 7 by 3 in. plates, and to each pair of posts fix a framed king-post truss, as shown in section, with $\frac{3}{4}$-in. iron bolt to king-post, and 1-in. camber to beam.

Fix collars 5 by 2 in. to driving way roof at each pair of posts, and fix braces 3 by 3 in. from each post to plates to support the same.

To the principal rafters nail 6 by $2\frac{1}{2}$ in. purlins, and fix cleats to same; and drive in, 3 in. apart, on the upper side of purlins, $1\frac{1}{2}$ in. large-headed galvanised nails, to prevent contact of boards with purlins when nailed on.

Cover the roofs with 7 by 1 in. boards $\frac{1}{4}$ in. apart, each board to have a groove, $\frac{1}{2}$ in. wide by $\frac{3}{8}$ in. deep, on the upper face, $\frac{1}{2}$ in. from each edge.

Form gutters 9 in. wide with 1-in. boards on 7 by 2 in. bearers well pitched inside, the plates having been fixed with a fall of 1 in. in 10 ft. to discharge the same to down-pipes; and form eaves troughs to sides in similar manner, 5 in. wide at bottom, supported by 6 by $1\frac{1}{2}$ in. brackets 4 ft. apart fixed to the braces between the posts.

Fix down-pipes 3 by 3 inside, of 1-in. boards, to discharge into pipes at ground level.

## Modern Farm Buildings:

### ESTIMATE OF COST OF THE WOOD ROOFS AT FIG. 30.

*Materials* (all timber creosoted).

| | £ | s. | d. |
|---|---|---|---|
| 150 ft. cube in-posts, at 3s. | 22 | 10 | 0 |
| 248 ft. cube in-plates, tie beams, king-posts, struts, principal rafters, purlins, ridge collars, braces, and hanging pieces for shutters, at 2s. | 24 | 16 | 0 |
| 11¾ square 7 by 1 in. boards for gutters and gables, at 14s. 6d. | 8 | 10 | 4 |
| 41 square 7 by 1 in. grooved roof and ridge boarding, at 15s. 6d. | 31 | 15 | 6 |
| Nails, bolts, nuts, and hinges | 3 | 8 | 6 |

*Labour.*

| | £ | s. | d. |
|---|---|---|---|
| 150 ft. cube fixing posts, at 3d. | 1 | 17 | 6 |
| 248 ft. cube framing and fixing timber in roof, at 6d. | 6 | 4 | 0 |
| 41 squares boarding to roof and ridge, at 2s. 6d. | 5 | 2 | 6 |
| 11¾ squares upright boarding to gables, including making and fixing gutters and shutters, at 4s. | 2 | 7 | 0 |
| Total | £106 | 11 | 4 |

This, for the 348 yards of ground covered, would be 6s. 2d. per superficial yard.

The foregoing iron and wood roofs, both superior of their kind, having been described, and the cost ascertained, it will be well to see how far it is practicable to reduce their cost by using less expensive (but of course less durable) materials, or otherwise.

The curved iron shedding costing 6s. 7d. per yard would admit of a saving in connection with the posts. If larch, in the round, was procurable from the estate, peeled, and the ends charred, the selling value of which might be put at 7s. 6d. each, a saving of £15 would be effected, or 10d. per superficial yard; and if the boarded gable ends were omitted, a further sum of about £7. 10s. would be gained, or 5d. per yard, thus reducing the 6s. 7d. to 5s. 4d., which accords with the price of several such roofs which I have erected. It would be scarcely possible to further lessen the cost, except by having a lighter gauge of iron, but this could not be recommended in the case of a curved roof.

The wooden roof would also admit of modifications by the substitution of similar larch posts, and the omission of the creosoted boarded gables. This would reduce the cost in a similar way from 6s. 2d. per yard to about 4s. 10d. per yard of ground covered. A further reduction might be made by using non-creosoted roof timbers, but this of course would be very undesirable, as decay would ensue within a few years in the case of a boarded roof of this description.

The form and construction of the wooden roof is, however, adaptable for the use of flat corrugated iron, instead of boards; and in this case, as the iron roof would be impervious to rain, the roof timbers need not be creosoted. A barn or shedding of this kind would be cheaper than any of the foregoing, as well as a lasting one, and the cost for the same sized erection would be as follows:—

*Materials.*

| | £ | s. | d. |
|---|---|---|---|
| 20 posts, at 7s. 6d. | 7 | 10 | 0 |
| 240 ft. cube of roofing timber, at 1s. 6d. | 18 | 0 | 0 |
| Flat corrugated iron, 22-in. gauge, to cover area of 348 yards, at 1s. 9d. | 30 | 9 | 0 |
| Bolts, nuts, nails, &c. | 5 | 0 | 0 |
| Eaves troughing and down-pipes | 5 | 0 | 0 |
| Iron ridge capping, 150 ft. | 2 | 0 | 0 |
| Total | £67 | 19 | 0 |

*Labour.*

| | £ | s. | d. |
|---|---|---|---|
| Fixing posts | 1 | 17 | 6 |
| 240 ft. cube framing and fixing roof timbers, at 6d. | 6 | 0 | 0 |
| 41 squares fixing iron, at 1s. 9d. | 3 | 11 | 9 |
| Fixing eaves troughing | 2 | 0 | 0 |
| Total | £81 | 8 | 3 |

This would amount to 4s. 8d. per yard for the 348 yards of ground covered ; or if the pitch of the roof (given for boards) was reduced, as it might be, the cost might be taken at 4s. 6d. per yard. This is the cheapest form of roofing, which is durable, for farm purposes.

But in addition to the question of the cost of the iron *versus* wooden, roofs, there is the important matter of suitability to be considered. Iron roofs have, of course, the advantage over the wooden roofs, constructed on the principle described, of being thoroughly water-tight ; and as a dry store is needed for grain, hay, and implements, iron is preferable for these, or for what is usually known as " dead farming stock." But for covered cattle-yards (and in a less degree for open cattle-shedding) the creosoted boarded roofs with $\frac{1}{4}$-in. openings, which admit some light and give good ventilation, are to be preferred, as being more healthy for cattle. They are cooler in summer, and the small amount of wet admitted through the $\frac{1}{4}$-in. apertures is of no material consequence; but I find that, when fixing the boards, an allowance for shrinkage must be made, or the apertures will be too large. There is very little difference between the cost of the one or the other, as shown by the examples, the iron being 6s. 7d. per yard, and the wood 6s. 2d. ; but it should be borne in mind that where large spans are required to save the cost of posts and their inconvenience, the wood roofs would be almost out of the question ; and in the case of large spans, supported by adjacent buildings, it is obvious that iron roofs would be cheaper.

As to the respective durability of iron and creosoted wood, I am satisfied that the former would be serviceable under ordinary circumstances for from thirty to forty years, and I see no reason why the latter should not be the same. The appearance of roofs have sometimes to be taken into

## Their Construction and Arrangement.

consideration, and it must be admitted that the soft hue of the creosoted boards is much more pleasing to the eye than the plain iron; but when the latter is cheaply and roughly painted a dark red colour with common oxide paint, it is not only unobjectionable but looks very well indeed.

I need not refer again to the modified and cheaper roofs which are shown to cost just below 5s. per yard of ground covered, but I may add that, at the time of writing, corrugated iron is quoted to me at £15 per ton (having of late considerably risen in price), and as a ton of 22-in. gauge will cover about 150 yards, it is now 2s. per yard for that strength. For 24-in. gauge the price would be about 1s. 9d. per yard, and if tenants can prevail upon their landlords (if they cannot do more) to allow them the timber for any roofing they require, they will find that the cost of the iron and labour of erection for Dutch barns would be repaid to them in a very few years by the saving in thatching and damaged corn, as well as in other respects connected with their general utility. This much may at least be said without attempting to enter upon the thorny question of negotiations between landlords and tenants which cannot be properly settled upon hard and fast lines, but are better disposed of on their individual merits.

## CHAPTER XIII.

### FARMHOUSES.

IT is desirable that both the agent of an estate and the clerk of works should be acquainted with the *requirements* of a farmhouse, in connection with which a good many details are involved, as it is better to be able to form an independent judgment than to have to rely on the ideas of the tenants, which too often run in special grooves. It is not intended, however, to deal with the details of construction in the same manner as has been done in regard to the parts of the homestead, but rather to call attention to altered conditions in the domestic arrangements of farm tenants, so far as they are likely to affect building operations. Some examples, however, of small farmhouses are given in the next chapter.

A builder cannot hide his mistakes in the proverbial way attributed to the medical profession, "six feet under ground"; they will always remain in evidence; and my advice will be the same as it was in the matter of farm buildings, to study not only the wants of the present occupier, but to look ahead and study the tendency of the times, as the modification of old farmhouses, to bring them up to present ideas and requirements, may sometimes involve as much change as a similar treatment of farm buildings. Such altered conditions as exist, or are likely to arise under modern farming practice, so far as they affect the farmhouse, should therefore be sought out, and I will call attention to some of them. In many districts it was formerly a common custom, but one now falling into disuse, for farmers to board and lodge their workmen; and where such has been the case, you may see what would now be considered abnormally large kitchens, and a large amount of inferior bedroom accommodation. It is quite possible that the more modern ideas of our farmers' wives have assisted to extinguish this old custom, but those who are acquainted with the ideas and general habits of living attaching to the "Hodge" of recent years, can scarcely blame these good ladies for their share in his banishment. Then as regards the communication with towns, before this was made easy by the railway system, many farmhouses were so remotely situated that neither the butchers', bakers', nor grocers' carts approached them, consequently they needed to be made independent of such supplies, hence the huge working apartments provided for brewing, salting and drying meat, baking, &c. But now farming life from a domestic point of view is more akin to that in the towns, and more frequently than otherwise baking and brewing are discarded altogether. It is in this respect that we may expect, by curtailment, to effect a saving, which will probably be wanted to meet the extra space and comfort now needed to bring the sitting-room department up to the standard of modern ideas, and also in dairy districts to provide for improved accommodation for dairy work and appliances.

The size of a farmhouse should be governed by the amount of rent of a farm rather than by its acreage, as it is obvious that 100 acres of land at £2 per acre will absorb more capital than the same amount at half the value; and the amount of capital at a tenant's disposal will be a safer guide than any other to his position in the social scale and the requirements of his household. At the same time, the rent received will be the natural basis for the agent's calculation for outlay in building. This rule, however, has sometimes been departed from by putting an extra good house on a farm of inferior quality, with a view of letting it more easily and to greater advantage, but it is only in times of great competition and prosperity that an extra outlay of this kind is likely to prove remunerative and serviceable.

As a rule, it is better to underbuild than otherwise, as it is possible in the case of most farmhouses, from the fact of their being detached, to make an addition when needed; and most tenants are aware of the extra expense attached to a house which is larger than is necessary, and do not care to have one. On a farm of £100 a year rental, a sitting-room, kitchen, scullery, dairy, and four bedrooms would probably suffice. A rental of £200 might need a parlour and one more bedroom in addition. For a £300 rental the parlour and sitting-room may be of a better class, and six bedrooms provided. Then in the case of £400 to £500 a year, it becomes a question of dining and drawing rooms, with a small sitting-room or office in addition, and a W.C. In the absence of any special considerations, these calculations may be taken as a general guide for the extent of accommodation required.

As regards site, if possible arrange that a window from the ordinary living-room shall command a view of the working parts of the homestead—it need not of course be the principal window of the apartment. Allow no drains to enter any part of the house, but let all discharges fall on to trapped gullies outside, particularly as regards the dairy. It is in the working apartments of the house—that is, the kitchen and scullery department—where mistakes are more likely to occur, and to be the source of grumbling on the part of the tenants, whose wives have perforce to spend much time there; and notwithstanding what has been said about a curtailment in some cases, in this department the opposite extreme should be avoided. No farmers' wives like to have the working apartments cramped, consequently the kitchen should be of ample proportions, and well lighted; and in small establishments it is sometimes desirable, on account of meals being often taken there, to be as large as those at larger houses. Instead of having the detached brewhouses, bakehouses, and wash-houses frequently met with, a well-arranged scullery forming part of the main building can now, owing to the considerations previously referred to, be made to serve for all these purposes. It should be lofty, and have ample means for getting rid of steam; and if separated from the other parts of the house by a passage or lobby, vapour and smells will be more effectually excluded. It is true that in some counties custom has left a preference for the buildings being detached where such rough work is carried on, but with care in arrangement I am convinced that no ill effects need be experienced where attachment to the house is made, while on the other hand considerable convenience accrues.

Farmers are sometimes hard to please in respect of the house they have to live in, and, rather than lose what may be thought to be a promising tenant, an agent may deem it prudent to offer to improve the appearance of the dwelling. It is, however, difficult to make a man who is ignorant of building matters understand how a mean and uninviting exterior can be improved and made to look pleasing and attractive, and on one occasion I should have lost a good man under such circumstances as these had I not promptly put an elevation before him showing what might be effected. There is a very trifling difference sometimes between the bare outlines of a church, a barn, and a house, and it is chiefly by means of windows, doors, and chimneys that the idea is conveyed as to what a building really is. By removing the meagre old lead windows, conveying as they did the idea of small and cheerless rooms, and replacing them with well-proportioned modern ones, by putting a good bold head to the chimney stacks, also a porch to the front door, and a small verandah, the exterior was rendered attractive to the tenant at a very moderate cost, and the idea conveyed of pleasanter and larger rooms within, and he was satisfied.

It is possible in the future, owing to the movement made in improving dairy produce, that more attention must be given to dairy accommodation. A later chapter will therefore be devoted to this part of the subject.

## CHAPTER XIV.

### HOMESTEADS FOR SMALL HOLDINGS.

OWING to the opinion which prevails to some extent in favour of the extension of small holdings, some attention may be given to their equipment with houses and buildings. Upon the advisability, or otherwise, of incurring expenditure for the purpose, I do not propose to dwell, as it is scarcely within the scope of this work. I have already discussed the matter from this point of view at some length elsewhere,* but it may be said here that, while admitting that there are some situations where a judicious outlay for the purpose appears to promise satisfactory results, it is advisable to recommend a cautious procedure, otherwise owners of farms which are difficult to let may be led into experiments of a costly nature, which will end in disappointment or financial failure.

The process of absorption of many small holdings by adjacent larger occupations is familiar to those whose experience carries them back prior to the commencement of the farming depression. It took place more particularly in arable districts, when there was a good demand for land at high rents, and landlords were thereby enabled to free themselves from the expense attached to maintaining small sets of farm buildings. Small owners also were desirous of turn-

\* See "Small Holdings and their Equipment," *Journal of the Royal Agricultural Society*, Third Series, vol. vii., Part II., 1896.

ing their freeholds into money to enable them to rent larger holdings when farming yielded good profits. But since low prices have lessened the demand for land generally, and have so materially reduced tenants' capital that it has become difficult to let large farms, it has become apparent to landlords in a good many cases that a mistake had been made in doing away with small farms. Public opinion has also been aroused by the migration of the rural population to the towns, and facilities have been given by the Legislature for the creation of small holdings under the auspices of County Councils; while the recommendation contained in a recent Report of the Royal Commission on Agriculture suggested that further financial facilities should be given for outlay of capital with the like object.

We thus see how the attention of landowners, and those interested in social problems of the kind, has been directed to the restoration of small holdings, and there is a fair prospect of success in certain localities for a very limited reintroduction of the principle. On the other hand, there is some fear that the zeal of more or less irresponsible enthusiasts may lead to the provision of small holdings which are doomed to failure.

Where it is thought desirable to subdivide a farm, the cost attached to the equipment of the land with buildings will, in most instances, be the main point to be considered; and it is obvious that if there are any outlying buildings, houses, or cottages on the farm, they should be inspected to ascertain whether they can be suitably adapted for small homesteads by additions or alterations, provided of course that the necessary land can be taken from the main holding without material detriment, and that when severed it will be fairly adapted for a small farm or farms—a matter which requires much discrimination.

Whatever the size may be of small farms, it is necessary to have the house and buildings adjoining or near to each other; and if a house or cottage exists which will be suitable of itself, or with some additions, half, or more than half, the difficulty as to outlay will be solved. If there are buildings also which can be adapted, so much the better; if not, these can be provided at a proportionately less cost than a house where this is a consideration, because wood and iron roofing can be economically employed for buildings, whereas dwelling-houses must be substantially built. It sometimes happens that outlying houses or buildings of this kind exist on large farms, being in some instances the remains, more or less neglected, of the small holdings which disappeared under the process before mentioned; and when this is the case it will be merely a matter of restoration and modernising to meet the requirements of the times, and the first thing will be to reckon the cost. The acreage of land proposed to be taken, its suitability for a small farm, and the rent likely to be obtained when a suitable homestead is provided, are also important factors. After summing up all the necessary expenditure, and considering what improved prospects there may be of letting the remainder of the farm, it will be possible to form an opinion whether the outlay is likely to be remunerative or otherwise.

The plans of a house and offices recently erected for a moderately small farm are shown at Figs. 32 to 35. It was designed by me to meet the requirements of a tenant who had just taken about 80 acres of land from a larger occupation which was found difficult to let satisfactorily, and it may be taken to represent fairly the requirements of ordinary working farmers paying a rental of about £100 a year. The farm buildings were situated on the right-hand side of

142

Fig. 32.

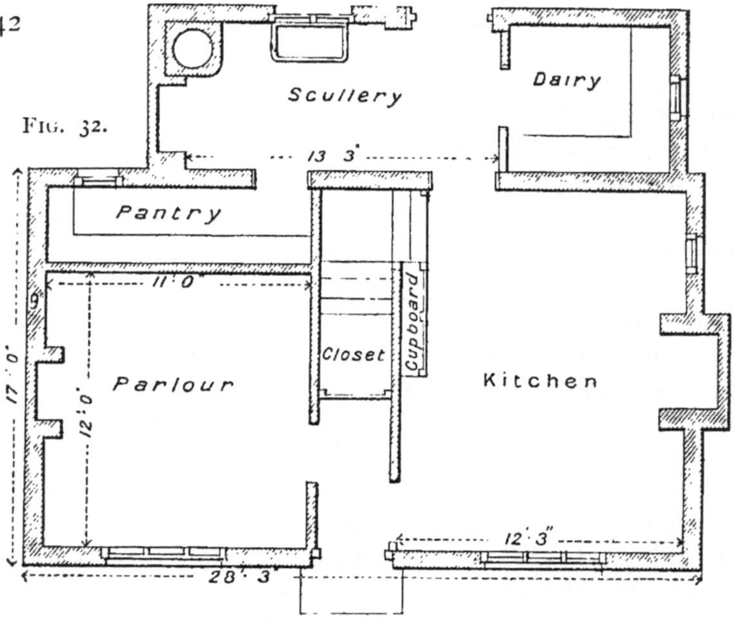

Ground Plan.

Fig. 33.

Chamber Plan.

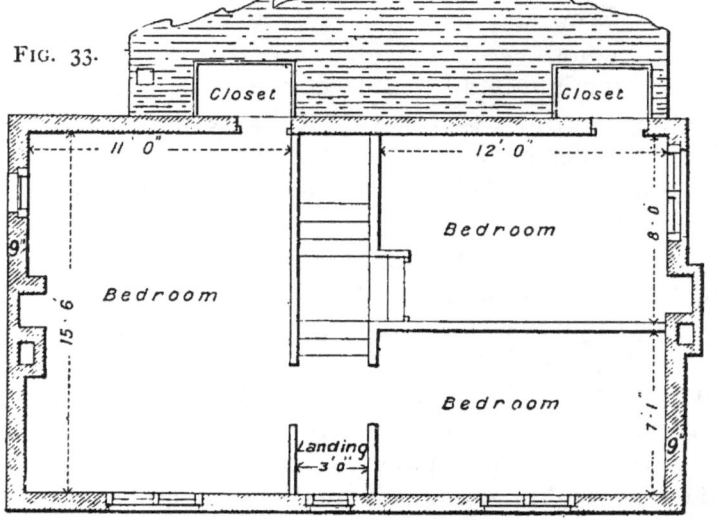

143

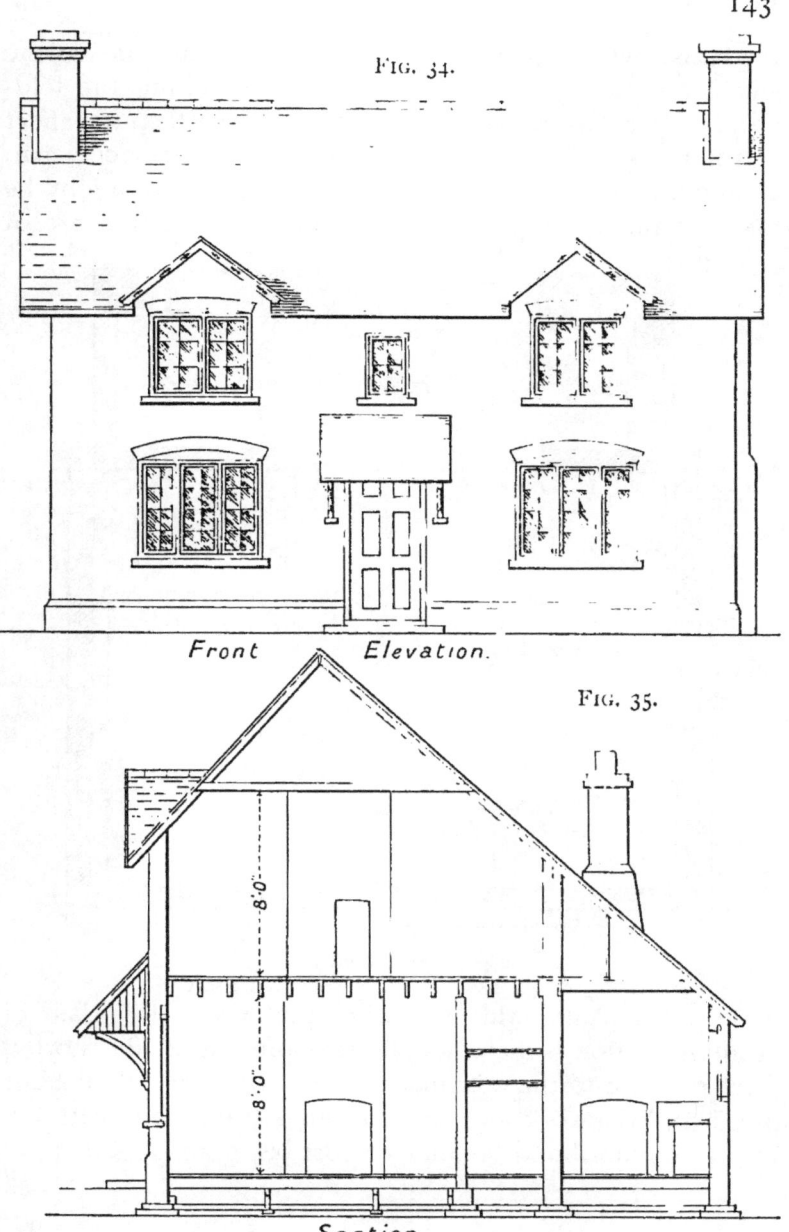

Fig. 34.

Front Elevation.

Fig. 35.

Section

the house, with an occupation road intervening; hence the small window put in the kitchen for overlooking the fold-yard. Cost having to be considered, architectural effect was not possible, and by getting the house under one span of roofing, economy was effected. Objection might be taken to there being only three bedrooms, but they are of

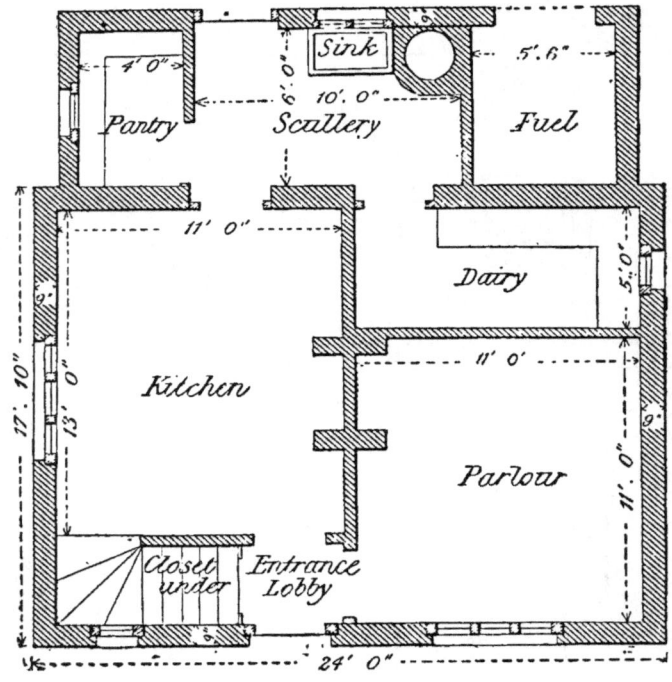

FIG. 36.—Ground Plan.

good size, and experience teaches that where this class of accommodation is more ample, it is often used for storing farm produce to the detriment of the structure. It is built of 9-inch brickwork and tiled, and has been found satisfactory to landlord and tenant, the cost being about £300.

## Their Construction and Arrangement. 145

Figs. 36 to 43 show the plans for a small house and buildings for a new complete homestead, which I recently designed, with several others, to accompany an article on "Small Holdings and their Equipment" in the *Royal Agricultural Society's Journal*, previously referred to, and it is hoped that they will serve, as some plans of larger

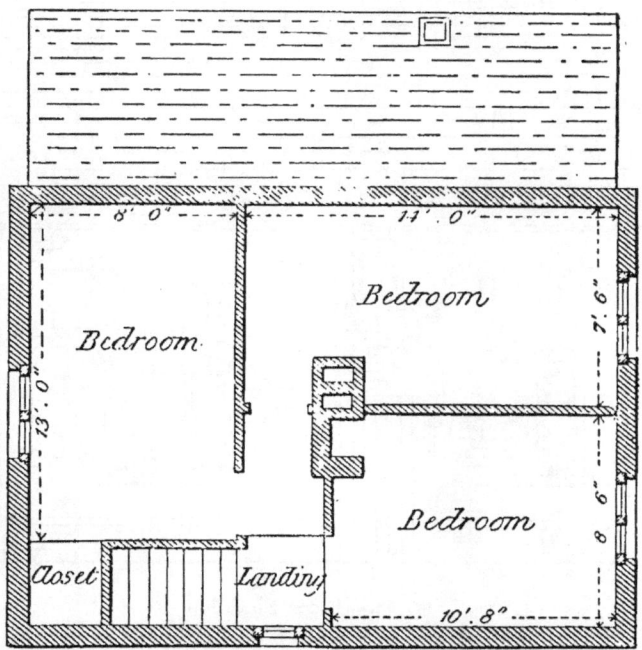

FIG. 37.—Chamber Plan.  House for Small Farm.

homesteads have done, to illustrate general principles of construction and arrangement, which can be modified in various ways to meet special requirements. I am indebted to the Society for permitting the reproduction of the homestead here; and as the article was written so recently as

K

in 1896, the matter, from the author's point of view, is up to date.

FIG. 38.—Front Elevation.

The house, shown by Figs. 36 to 39, cannot be more serviceably described than by quoting from the article in question :—

"It may be considered suitable for any farm from 20 acres to 50 acres ; or even in some cases it might serve for 100 acres of land, because it is often more a question of rent, of tenant's capital employed, and of the class of land, than size, which has to be considered.

## Their Construction and Arrangement. 147

As there is a small parlour in this design, in addition to the living room or kitchen, the scullery has been reduced to the smallest possible dimensions, because the kitchen can be used more freely for the work of the house to the relief of the latter where there is a better room for occasional use. The scullery, pantry, and fuel place are only of

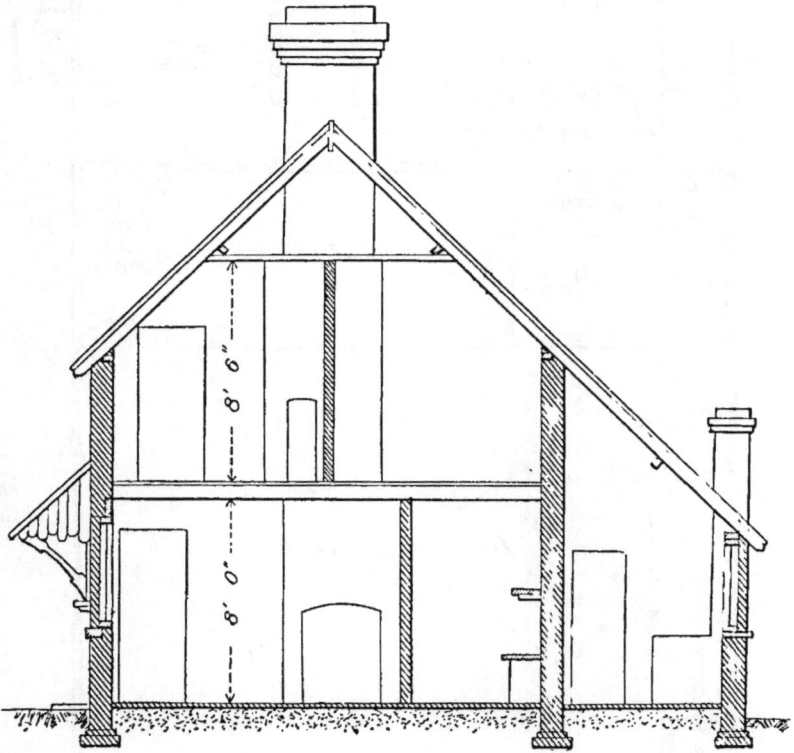

FIG. 39.—Section. House for Small Farm.

one storey, in the form of a lean-to. One-storey buildings do not conduce to building economy as a rule, but in this case they are inevitable, as the accommodation given on the ground floor is all wanted, and I did not consider that more than the three bedrooms given on the upper floor was needed. In fact a fourth bedroom is usually objectionable

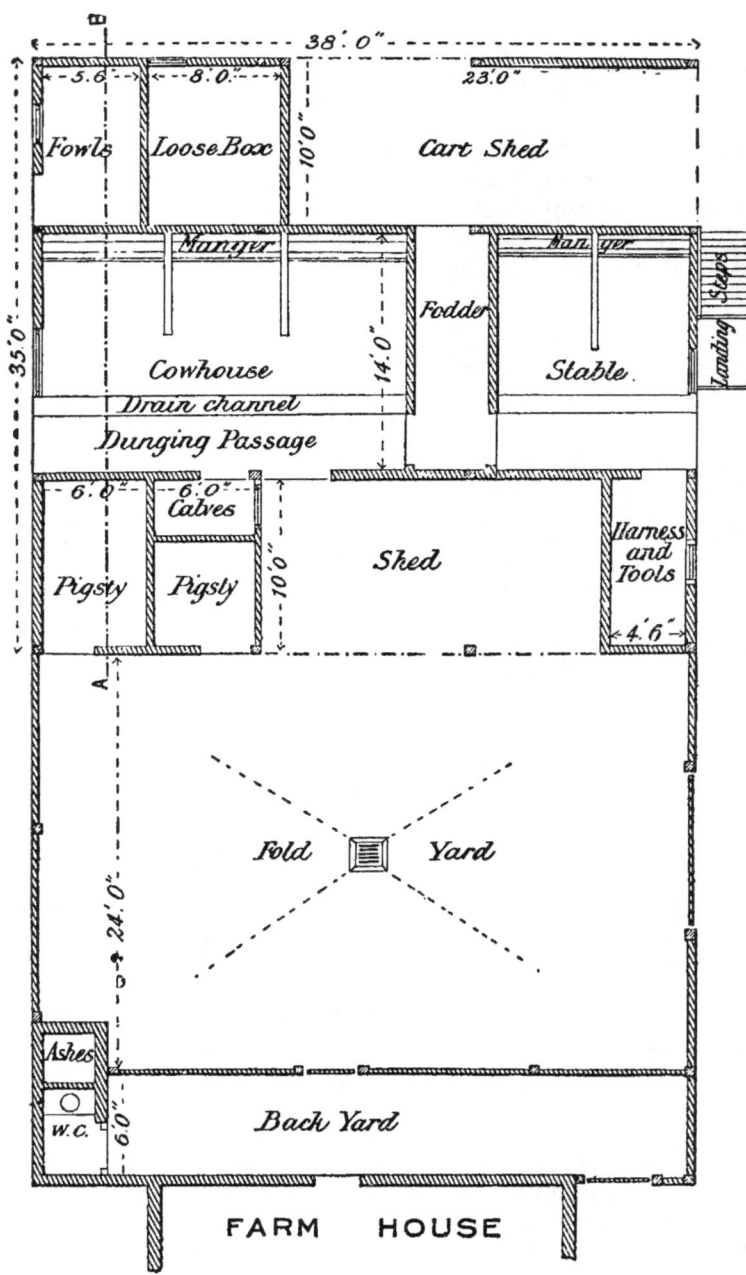

Fig. 40.—Ground Plan. Homestead for Small Farm.

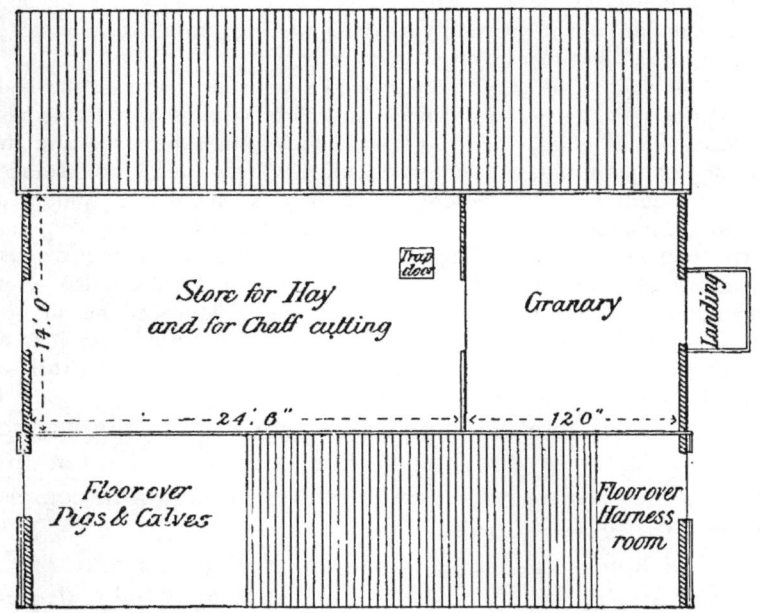

Fig. 41.—Plan of Upper Storey.

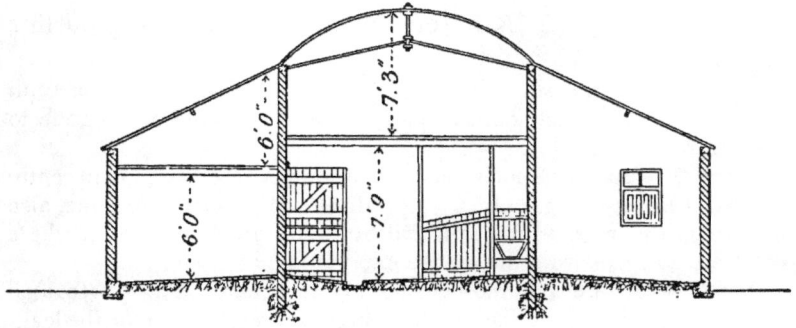

Fig. 42.—Section along A B in Fig 40 opposite. Homestead for Small Farm.

in such houses as these, as when not absolutely required for sleeping accommodation it is invariably used for storing grain, fruit, or vegetables, to the detriment of the structure.

"The superficial area on the ground floor is 485 feet; on the bedroom floor 362 feet; and the whole structure contains 9,477 cubic feet Houses of this class, brick and tiled, I find from experience and the pricing of quantities, can under moderately favourable circumstances be well built for 4¾d. per foot, which in this case would amount to £187. This sum should cover the cost of a well (if not very deep); a privy such as placed adjoining the fold-yard of Fig. 40, where this house is shown attached to a homestead; and it should allow also a few pounds for garden fencing. The cost might, however, be slightly reduced by using slates on a lower pitched roof, but otherwise it is as moderate as it can be made without resorting to 'jerry built' work, or unduly curtailing the efficiency of the structure."

As the principles which should govern the building of farmhouses were discussed in the preceding chapter, this part of the subject need not be referred to again in connection with these examples.

The homestead shown in plan at Figs. 40 and 41, in section at Fig. 42, and as a "view" at Fig. 43, will also be best described in the terms of the article. The arrangement in a single block under one roof has been selected for economy; and to attain this to a greater degree, corrugated iron and timber are used. The points of construction will be best understood by a reference to the following outline specification:—

*Site.*—Level the site for the buildings and to a distance of 12 ft. around them, and dish out the fold-yard with a fall of 6 in. in 10 ft. to the centre.

*Drains.*—Build cesspools outside stable and cow-house, and in centre of yard. Lay 4-in. agricultural pipe drains to connect the same, also to take up the water from roofs, and carry the drain to a point where directed, 20 yards from the cesspool in yard.

*Posts.*—Prepare and mortice eight 7-in. square oak, or creosoted deal posts, for two-storey central building; and eight ditto for the lean-to buildings, and well ram the same in the ground with concrete.

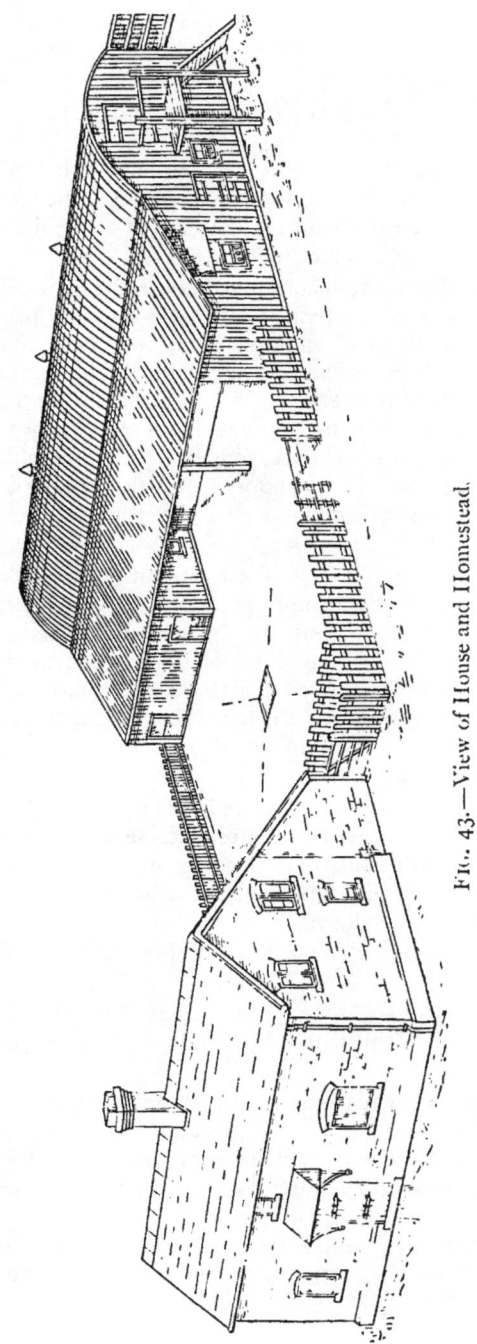

FIG. 43.—View of House and Homestead.

151

"*Brick Foundation.*—Dig trench, and build 9-in. brick dwarf-wall on one course of 14-in. work, as shown in section, to be finished with brick on edge in cement, all round the exterior of the buildings to prevent rotting of timbers at ground line.

"*Paving.*—Pave the whole space covered by the buildings (except cart-shed and shed to fold-yard) with hard building brick laid in sand, on 6 in. of dry rubble well rammed, and grout the same with mortar; the floor of stable to be laid on edge and the remainder flat; and all with necessary falls to the drain-channels, which are to be 12 in. wide.

"*Flooring.*—Fix 7 in. by 3 in. deal joists on 7 in. by 3 in. beams morticed into posts, over cow-house, fodder-store, and stable, and lay 1-in. boarding on same to form the upper storey floor; also fix 5 by 3 beams with 1-in. boarding to form floors over pigsty and harness-room to hold litter for the cattle.

"*Walls.*—All walls, except the partition on upper floor, to be constructed with rails $3\frac{1}{2}$ by $2\frac{1}{2}$, not exceeding 1 ft. 9 in. apart, braces where required $3\frac{1}{2}$ by $2\frac{1}{2}$, door jambs $4\frac{1}{2}$ by 4, and the same to be covered with 'space' boarding 1 in. thick—*i.e.*, boards nailed on rails 5 in. apart and the aperture covered with boards 7 in. wide, so as to give additional strength to the structure and prevent openings by shrinkage. The division on upper floor to be of ordinary inch boarding on $3\frac{1}{2}$ by $2\frac{1}{2}$ studs and braces.

"*Doors.*—All doors to be $1\frac{1}{4}$ in. ledged and braced, hung with strong strap hinges and in halves where on outside of cow-house and stable. Pigsties to have half doors only, leaving aperture above.

"*Windows.*—Hit-and-miss windows, with upper part of strong rolled glass, to be put where shown.

"*Mangers.*—Mangers to be formed of $1\frac{1}{2}$-in. deal, with oak chin rail, on strong supports.

"*Stall Divisions.*—To have 4 by 4 posts let into floor and fastened to floor joists above. Rail with 4 by 3 rails, and board one side with $1\frac{1}{4}$-in. boards.

"*Roofs.*—Roofs to be formed of 22-gauge corrugated iron, with a circular span in centre on $4\frac{1}{2}$ by 3 plates and one set of tie rods, and the lean-to sides of flat sheets, tied in from post to post with 5 by $2\frac{1}{2}$ battens: $4\frac{1}{2}$-in. half-round spouting to be fixed to eaves with four down-pipes.

"*Landing and Steps.*—Fix two 5 by 5 oak posts or creosoted deal in ground in concrete, and form landing and steps as shown. Put upright ladder from fodder-house to floor above, and form trap-door above the same.

"*Tarring.*—Tar all outside woodwork with two coats of tar.

"*Fencing.*—Fence fold-yard with 5 by 5 oak posts, 6 by 7 gate-posts, 3½ by 2½ rails, and 4 by 1¼ pales, and hang a strong gate and wicket where shown.

"The object of setting out this class of building is to meet the exigencies of the times in the matter of expense; but even in cases where this is not so important, it is questionable how far the erection of very substantial farm buildings is now justified, as it is impossible to foresee what changes may take place in the future which would render them more or less useless. This is the case, as we know, with many homesteads now on large farms, and owners are regretting that so much money had been expended upon them.

"But when a building is erected as here shown, in the form of a single block, so much structural economy is effected that it is possible to construct the outer walls with brick, and to cover the roofs with corrugated pantiles on boards, or with slates, at a comparatively small additional cost, as the walls are reduced to a minimum. The cost of the homestead built according to the specification, which provides for strong and good work of its class (a dwarf brick wall being carried up above the ground line all round to prevent the decay of the woodwork), I estimate to amount to £1 a yard of ground covered by the buildings, this price including the fencing in of the fold-yard ; and the area being 156 yards, the cost is £156. If the brick outer walls and tile or slate constructed roofs are substituted for the wood and iron, the price will be increased to £200, or by about 30 per cent. These are taken to be the contractor's prices under favourable conditions; but if the work is undertaken by estate workmen, and the resources of estate building yards are available for English timber which could be had at little cost, and other facilities, a saving on the prices named may of course be effected. The 'space' boarding described in the specification is well adapted for the use of English timber, and it is much stronger than the ordinary feather-edged weather boarding nailed on horizontally.

"As regards the accommodation given at the homestead it will be evident that, given a space enclosed and roofed in of 156 superficial yards of area on the most economical principles, it can be divided in many ways to meet particular requirements. I have assumed that, as now arranged, the buildings will meet the needs of an ordinary small farm of, say, 50 acres of land of moderate quality, mainly grass but with a little arable; or for 30 acres of more productive land which will carry the same amount of stock. Ten cows could be kept, six in the stalls, and four, when dry, in the yard; or fewer cows, and some young stock. The stable takes two horses, which is more than the farm work requires; but it is assumed that the occupier will add to his means of living by hauling for hire or working as a carrier. There is of course accommodation for pigs and fowls, and a useful feature will be found in the upper storey, which, in addition to its utility for the storage of grain and fodder, does away with the objection often raised to stock being housed directly under iron roofs on account of their transmitting both heat and cold too freely. Cross ventilation is easily introduced just under the upper floor, and if more than this is necessary, apertures could be made in the floor directly under the ventilators in the roof and connections made between them with wooden funnels.

"It will be seen, of course, that the cow-house can be extended, and the stable reduced, or the reverse; and the same may be done with the other parts as may be required. Working convenience and other points of advantage have been made the most of; the manure from the buildings can be taken direct into the yard, and it is advantageous to be able to turn cows, when untied, into a yard at once, as they invariably commence to dung as soon as they move. The shed and the pigsties have a southern aspect, and the latter opening into the yard, enables the pigs to be run out over the manure as required, and the same may be said of the calf-house. The floors over the pigsties are available for litter or various odds and ends, and as the sties are 6 ft. high inside, they are equally serviceable if required for young stock, or for many other purposes. The floor over the pigsties also keeps the pigs warmer than they would otherwise be."

Fig. 43 gives a "view" of the house and buildings just described, forming a complete homestead, costing respectively as estimated, £187 and £156; and an addition of £7 for roads and fences would make a sum of £350 for the whole.

Further example homesteads might be given if the importance of the subject rendered it necessary to do so. It will be sufficient, however, to direct attention to the adaptability of the plan of the iron roofed homestead, Figs. 40 to 43, for larger or smaller requirements, or for being built with more substantial materials. It is evident that the grouping of the buildings in a single block cannot well be improved upon, either on the grounds of economy in building, or in the working convenience of the occupier. The cow-house and the stable, with the store and granary above, can be enlarged by extensions, in which case the minor lean-to buildings would probably require extension also; or a reduction may be made by curtailment of the same.

The iron roofing may be objected to, and many persons might consider the timber walls to be insufficiently durable ; but at a time when rapid changes in all matters connected with land are as likely as not to occur, it will not always be wise to build too substantially. To meet these objections, however, the main, or two-storey portion, could be built with brick, leaving the lean-to portions as they are, or making them of brick also ; and in either case the outlines of the design could remain the same. Likewise, slates or tiles might be substituted for the iron roofing on the main building, and also on the lean-to portions; but except in the case of animals standing in an enclosed and shut up building, without an intervening chamber above them, there need be no objection to an iron roof. The stable, cow-house, and pigsties have floors above which serve to moderate the extremes of temperature arising from the iron, while the air circulating in open shedding with iron roofing will effect the same purpose ; and there is a further advantage attached to this class of roof resulting from the absence of the necessity for the replacement of tiles after high winds.

There are many remarks in other chapters which will apply equally to this section of the work on the details of fitting up the buildings and otherwise, therefore it is not necessary to repeat them here. One point, however, must not be overlooked, which is the sanitary requirements of the cow-houses in these small homesteads. Where wood is used for the sake of economy, a coating or two of tar applied occasionally to the interior will render the wood non-absorbent and keep the place healthy, provided the flooring is sound and ventilation good. This can be done at a small cost, and ought to satisfy all hygienic requirements where only two or three cows are kept.

There is a plan of a pair of cottages given in the next chapter which would be suitable, or otherwise adaptable for small holdings of a few acres where it is desirable to erect dwellings of that class.

## CHAPTER XV.

### COTTAGES.

IT is well known that the building of cottages in rural districts is not remunerative, if the small rents obtainable from labourers is the only consideration to set against the cost of erection. But farming work has to be done, and the labourers must be housed, and any direct loss must be set against the improved value of the land after it has been equipped with proper dwellings for the men who till it.

A great deal has been written on the subject, and in most land agents' offices numerous plans of cottages are pigeon-holed, many of which are probably of the ornamental kind, and it may be somewhat out of date, because they do not meet the requirements of the present day. I do not propose to add more than one plan to the number, but it is hoped that this will be found serviceable, and it need not be costly to build.

For obvious reasons, it is usually better to build pairs of cottages than single dwellings, and each dwelling requires at least, a living-room, small scullery, and a pantry on the ground floor; and for the separation of the sexes, three bedrooms above. Occasionally an elderly or young married couple can manage with two bedrooms, and a few of such cottages can be fairly placed amongst a number of others, but where erected on a farm it is much better to allow three rooms. This amount of accommodation is now

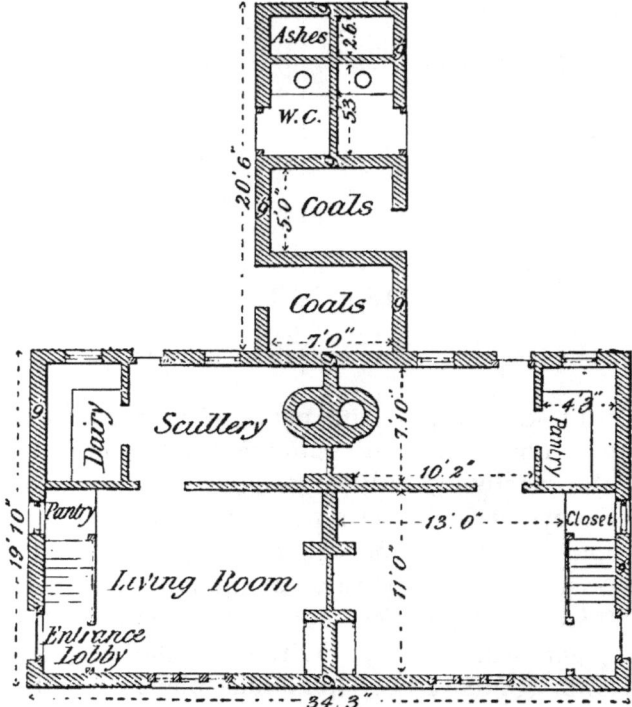

Fig. 44.—Ground Plan.

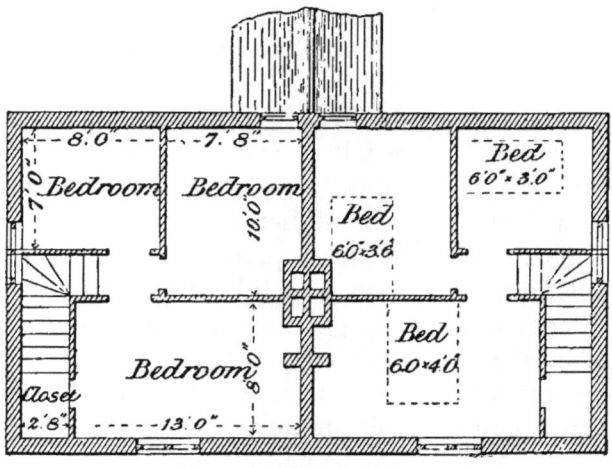

Fig. 45.—Chamber Plan.

PAIR OF COTTAGES.

159

Fig. 46.—Front Elevation.

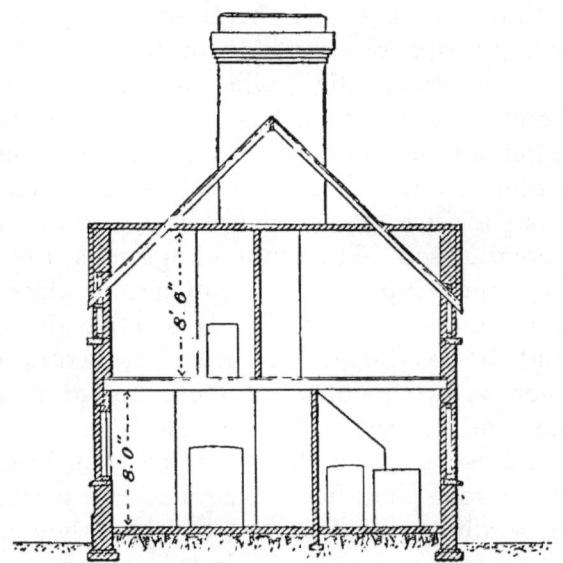

Fig. 47.—Section.
Pair of Cottages.

generally accepted as reasonable and necessary, but as there are many ways of arranging the rooms, staircases, windows, and other parts of the structure, the art of the designer will tell even in so small a matter as building a cottage. In small rooms, a badly-placed door, window, or projection will destroy comfort and convenience, and often renders a certain amount of area useless; whereas a well-arranged plan will be more economical to build if it provides, as it should do, the maximum of convenience on a minimum area. It is such a plan that I have endeavoured to furnish at Figs. 44 to 47, and it is identical with a design for a pair of cottages for small farms which accompanied my article in the *Royal Agricultural Society's Journal* referred to in the preceding chapter.

In the ground plan it will be seen that there is an entrance lobby, out of which the stairs start; the living-room has cupboards on one side of the fireplace and a closet under the stairs; the scullery has a fireplace on the hearth, a copper and a sink, but the brick oven which is now so seldom used is omitted. The three bedrooms above are of fair dimensions and of good height, a fireplace being placed in one for use in case of sickness, and in this room there is a good closet. The outbuildings consist of a coal-house, privy, and ashpit to each cottage, so placed as to divide the premises at the back. If pigsties are required, they should be placed farther from the cottages, and working men will frequently put these up for themselves if some cheap or old materials are given them.

As regards cost, the cottages are of 9-in. brick walls with flat-tiled roofs, and from experience of similar work done under ordinary conditions, I consider they could be built at $4\frac{1}{2}$d. per foot cube. This will amount to £282, including the cost of a well of moderate depth; and in confirmation of this it may be stated that a pair of cottages were recently erected in Bedfordshire from this design, with the exception of earth-closets being substituted for privies, and the owner informed me that they cost just under £300. They gave him every satisfaction, and he was much pleased with the arrangement of the outbuildings which gave privacy to the tenants at the back of the houses.

If, on the whole, the arrangement of the area built upon can be regarded as giving the maximum of serviceable accommodation in proportion to its size, which is the object which has been aimed at, there is no reason why the design should not be adapted for cottages of a more superior class, where needed, either by increasing the dimensions or by giving a more attractive elevation to harmonise with the surroundings, or to conform to any special requirements. For this purpose the roof could be broken up by means of valleys and large gables, porches placed over the entrances, string courses of various kinds of bricks provided, and ornamental windows; and many other features might be introduced without altering the essential arrangement of the interior. Or it may be that matters of constructive detail are required to be altered, such as the thickness of the 9-in. walls. This is sufficient for strength, and for resisting damp, if the bricks are hard and good, and a proper damp course of slates and cement is provided; otherwise 14-in. work, or hollow work of two $4\frac{1}{2}$-in. walls with a 2-in. cavity and iron ties 2 ft. apart every four courses will be advisable.

If for the sake of economising outlay it was desired to have one smaller cottage of two bedrooms only, attached to the larger one, the alteration could be conveniently effected by doing away with the staircase beside one of

L

the living-rooms and the pantry of the same cottage, and building the end wall some 3 ft. farther in. The staircase should then be fixed in the scullery against the end wall to land about the centre of the floor above where one partition would form two bedrooms. A small pantry could be formed under the stairs, while all the other arrangements, including the front elevation, would not be affected.

In cottage building, apart from the desirability of providing decent and comfortable homes for working men on philanthropic grounds, there is now a strong incentive for doing so, as a means of attracting labourers to the soil; and to put the matter on lower grounds, sanitary legislation, which has a tendency to become more stringent, has to be taken account of. Bearing these in mind, it does not seem advisable to curtail either the superficial or cubical area of the plans. Every precaution should be taken against dampness, and an aspect as nearly south as possible should be selected for the site. One slop drain for each cottage is all that is necessary, and these should be outside properly trapped, with the pipes from the sinks discharging upon them, and the drains should be carefully laid so as not to pollute the well or other water supply.

Where small houses in pairs are required for small holdings of land, the design will also, in some cases, be suitable. Hence a dairy is shown in one of the cottages (which in the other is given as a pantry), and a small pantry is placed under the stairs, in order to meet the requirements of cowkeeping.

## CHAPTER XVI.

### DAIRIES.

A VARIETY of circumstances, to which it is not necessary to refer, has now brought into greater prominence the methods of dealing with milk and its manufacture into butter and cheese than hitherto has been the case, but probably the competition now existing between foreign and home products has had the greater share in directing attention to improved practice in this respect.

It is necessary, in the first place, to keep milk perfectly pure, by placing it under such conditions that it cannot be contaminated by dirt or effluvia of any description, as it is now well understood that it is most susceptible to the presence of any impurities in the atmosphere or otherwise; secondly, some means of moderating the extremes of temperature are required to enable the maximum of cream to be extracted from the milk. These are the main objects to be aimed at in the construction of dairy buildings, and their appreciation can best be effected by a study of detail, which I will endeavour to supply.

The Royal Agricultural Society, by the liberality of the Surveyors' Institution, offered prizes at its Windsor Show for butter dairies, Messrs Thos. Bradford & Co. being successful. Their plans, reproduced here by permission, at Figs. 48 and 49, will serve as an excellent illustration of the details of construction required for the exercise of first-class dairy practice brought down to date.

It need scarcely be remarked, that those persons having the control of the building department of an estate will hardly ever be in a position, or think it advisable, to follow out the precise methods of construction and equipment shown by these designs; but the plans will be most serviceable as "text plans," illustrating desirable features and good points, which may be more or less attainable, in a sufficient degree, by the exercise of care and intelligence in readapting present structures needing the same, or in building new ones, without incurring undue expenditure. The object of the R.A.S.E. has doubtless been to obtain designs of a *perfect* dairy, as a means of educating those interested in such structures; and we cannot do better than study the plans which, in the opinion of the Society, most closely approached the standard of perfection.

Fig. 48 is a representation of Messrs Bradford's prize plan of a butter dairy for a farm under 100 acres. It is a completely detached building, facing the north, although capable of attachment to other buildings, and there is no reason why a dairy on this principle should not fulfil the purposes required for a much larger farm, if the "setting" of milk is practised. When the milk is brought in through the corridor it can be taken to the setting-room, which also serves as a store for the butter. A creaming apparatus, with cold-water fittings and jackets, is shown, in which the milk is placed, but instead of this slate or other shelves could be fixed to carry the milk-pans. This room serves for no other purposes, and the doorway does not communicate direct with any other apartment, these features being necessary for absolute cleanliness and freedom from taint. What is termed the "dairy" is a place for the working plant, making the butter, and washing the utensils. In an ordinary way the usual farmhouse dairy has to serve for these rooms in the plan, and with scrupulous care they will answer very well, but it is obvious that perfect cleanliness and purity cannot be attained where other domestic work is carried on. The boiler-room, however, which

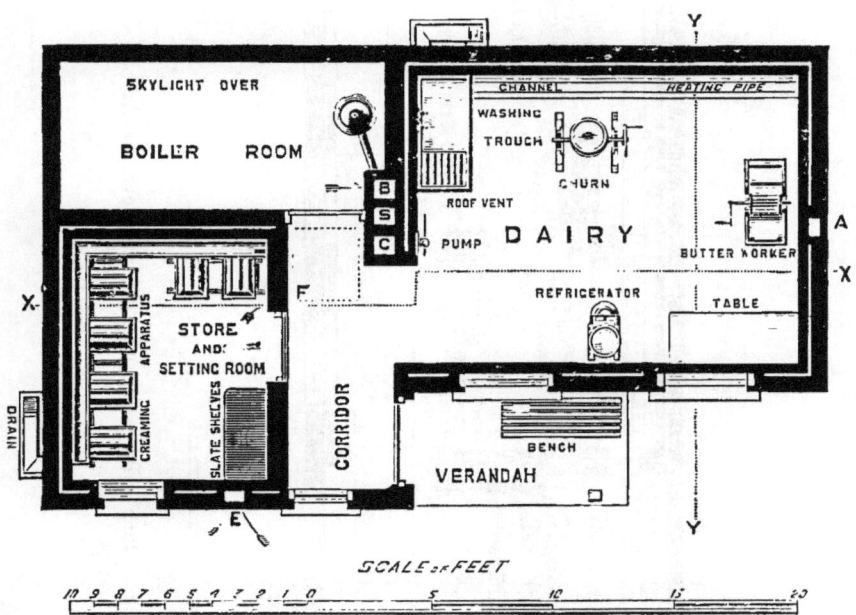

FIG. 48.—Plan of Butter Dairy for a Farm of under 100 Acres.

contains heating and cold-water apparatus, is a distinct addition to ordinary dairy equipment, and serves a very useful purpose in connection with washing up and heating the rooms in winter, which, to ensure the best results, require to be kept at a temperature of about 60°. The verandah is fitted with a bench for draining and sweetening the cans and utensils by exposure to the air.

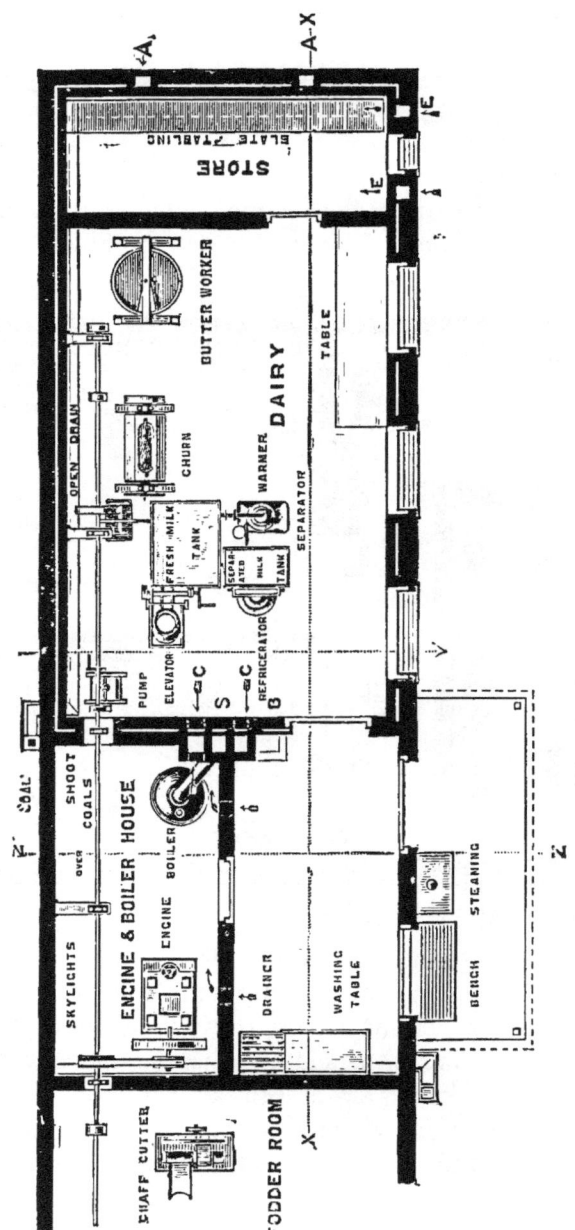

FIG. 49.—Plan of Butter Dairy for a Farm of over 100 Acres.

The other design, Fig. 49, is a prize plan of the butter dairy for a farm of over 100 acres, also by Messrs Bradford, and consequently may be adapted for a very large dairy. At its present size it is suited for 80 or 100 cows, and, like the previous design, it faces the north. It is shown as being attached to the fodder-room of the farm buildings, which enables it to avail of the steam power used in connection with food preparation. The arrangement of the four rooms in this design is on the assumption that, instead of setting the milk for cream to rise, it would be refrigerated or warmed, as might be necessary, when brought in, and separated. The dairy, which is the working apartment, is adapted for these operations, including of course the churning, which could be done almost daily, therefore a comparatively small room is required, as shown, as a store for the butter. The engine-house is fitted with a boiler of 4 horse-power and an engine of 2 horse-power, and provides room for the storage of coal, while the scullery, which is devoted to washing-up purposes, serves to sever communication with the other rooms, and so avoid injury to milk or butter by bad smells. A verandah is applied to the same use as that in the smaller design, with a steaming jet for cleansing purposes in addition.

The chief interest and importance of these plans, as would be the case with any other dairy buildings which aspired to be thoroughly effective, centres naturally in the details of their construction, and as they are regulated by the same principles in both designs, they can be treated of together. The north aspect for all the windows is, of course, shown. The walls (except of the boiler-house) are 14 in., with a cavity to minimise heat in summer and cold in winter. There seems to be no reason, however, why a 9-in. wall with a cavity, tied in with iron ties 2 ft. apart in every fourth course, should not be sufficient. The roofs are of slate, but most persons consider tiles are preferable. Thatch, however, is the most perfect material, as it modifies the extremes of temperature to a greater extent than either. The rooms are ceiled with match-boarding and varnished, and the space between the ceiling and the roof is ventilated, which is an excellent plan.

The ventilation in both designs appears to have been well arranged. There are extracting flues, C, situated beside the smoke flue, S, so that the air in the former would be warmed by the latter, and an upward current maintained. These ventilating flues would extract air from the dairies close under the ceiling where the warmest air would be. In the store-rooms there are inlet flues at E to admit fresh air on the north side, which are fitted with regulators, and from these the air will pass through openings into the dairies, the current in each case being maintained through both rooms by the extracting flues C previously mentioned. The boiler-houses and cleaning-room will also be ventilated into the extracting flues C; and the designers remark, that if local conditions were favourable, the fresh air for the inlet flues E could be brought through an underground culvert so as to cool the air in transit.

The heating in winter would, in the case of Fig. 49, be carried out by a steam pipe carried along the walls and regulated by a valve; and in the case of Fig. 48, by an apparatus from the boiler-room arranged with hot-water pipes carried round the walls, one fire acting for this and the supply of hot water.

The floors would be either cement or flags, according to the locality, with open channels for drainage discharging on to gullies outside. This is an important provision, as under no circumstances ought a cesspit or gully to be placed inside any dairy buildings. The upper part of the windows are made to open inwards, the space outside being covered with gauze.

As regards the fitting up of the design for about 100 cows, it will be seen that a number of modern appliances are to be used by means of steam power, which is provided for use in common with the preparation of food. On a farm of this size, as also on those considerably smaller, where the steam power can thus be used for two purposes, the system is no doubt a labour-saving and profitable one. On being brought in, the milk is delivered by a mechanical elevator into the milk storage tank, situated on a raised platform. It would then gravitate over the milk-warmer into the separator, which would be capable of separating ninety gallons per hour. The separated milk would be then mechanically raised to a small tank, to flow over a refrigerator into delivery cans or a milk vat.

If the milk is to be stored for the night before it is separated, the elevator can be placed in position for refrigerating it before being stored. The churn, butter-worker, and making-up table merely require to be mentioned as being worked also from the same shaft, as also is the pump, and there is a cold-water storage tank in the roof.

In the setting-room and store, it is worthy of note that the slate shelves are fixed at a slight distance from the wall for the better circulation of air. White tiles are recommended for lining the walls to a height of 4 ft. 6 in. from the floor for ensuring cleanliness. As a cheaper substitute, however, I have found that ordinary red quarries answer the purpose very well.

A perusal of these excellent designs in which dairy

practice "up to date" is so clearly illustrated, cannot fail to instruct, and be of some use to all persons interested in the subject. There does not appear to be much room for adverse criticism, but still there are one or two features which may be open to objection. It does not seem desirable, for obvious reasons, that the only approach to the boiler-rooms should be through the other rooms although in Fig. 48 it is only a corridor; and it would seem that, when windows can be introduced east and west as well as north, it would be an advantage to introduce them for creating a stronger current of air through the rooms than the ventilators can provide. Such windows could be protected by shutters, or by planting shrubs to exclude the sun's rays. As regards the verandahs, I think, where possible, that it is advisable to place them outside the south walls, for modifying the action of the sun upon them, and also for exposing to the sun (as a purifier) the appliances after being washed. Any alterations, however, as regards these matters could easily be made in the designs, but in building in connection with any particular site, local considerations would, of course, be brought into bearing.

The policy of regulating the temperature of dairies will be appreciated when we consider that uniformity of temperature is regarded by practical men as a material element of success, some fixing the desired degree at a little over, and some a little less, than 60° Fahr. Its influence seems to be placed beyond all doubt by the evidence of Mr Horsfall, a dairy farmer of repute, who says:—"By a series of carefully conducted experiments, I am of opinion that a correct scale of the comparative yield of butter at different temperatures might be arrived at—thus, from a temperature of about 38°, 16 oz. from

16 quarts of milk; ditto, 45', 21 oz. from 16 quarts of milk; ditto, 55°, 26 to 27 oz. from 16 quarts of milk."

As previously remarked, the designs submitted must be looked upon, as far as ordinary practice goes, as text plans which embody facilities for carrying out the most scientifically correct dairy practice; but it will be admitted that, while it may be necessary to adhere to the more primitive arrangement of one apartment for the dairy, and the use of the scullery for cleaning utensils—and such will be the case in a majority of instances—there are many features of the designs which can be reproduced with advantage, and at moderate cost, when occasion arises for renovating this part of a farm homestead.

## CHAPTER XVII.

### POULTRY HOUSES.

ACCOMMODATION for poultry is a modest, though necessary, adjunct to all farm homesteads. The busy farmer himself pays little attention as a rule to the feathered tribe, but a thrifty wife knows too well the profit attached to them, even if she had to buy all the food required in addition to that which they can pick up. There can be no doubt about this, although so much cannot be said as regards the profit of poultry farms pure and simple, which are not successful.

Plans of poultry houses, and even of elaborate "poultry steadings," have been given from time to time in various works devoted solely to the feathered tribe, and for an exhaustive study of the subject one or more of these should be referred to; but as the desire usually is at a farmery that moderate accommodation should be given, in one or two houses, for the various descriptions of fowls usually kept, the object here will be to keep within this limit.

The attendance on fowls is so disconnected with the ordinary work at a homestead, and the buildings required are of such moderate dimensions, that they can be placed at almost any place which may be thought suitable as regards site and aspect. When the attendance is given by the farmer's wife or daughter they should be of easy access from the house; yet, on the other hand, proximity to the

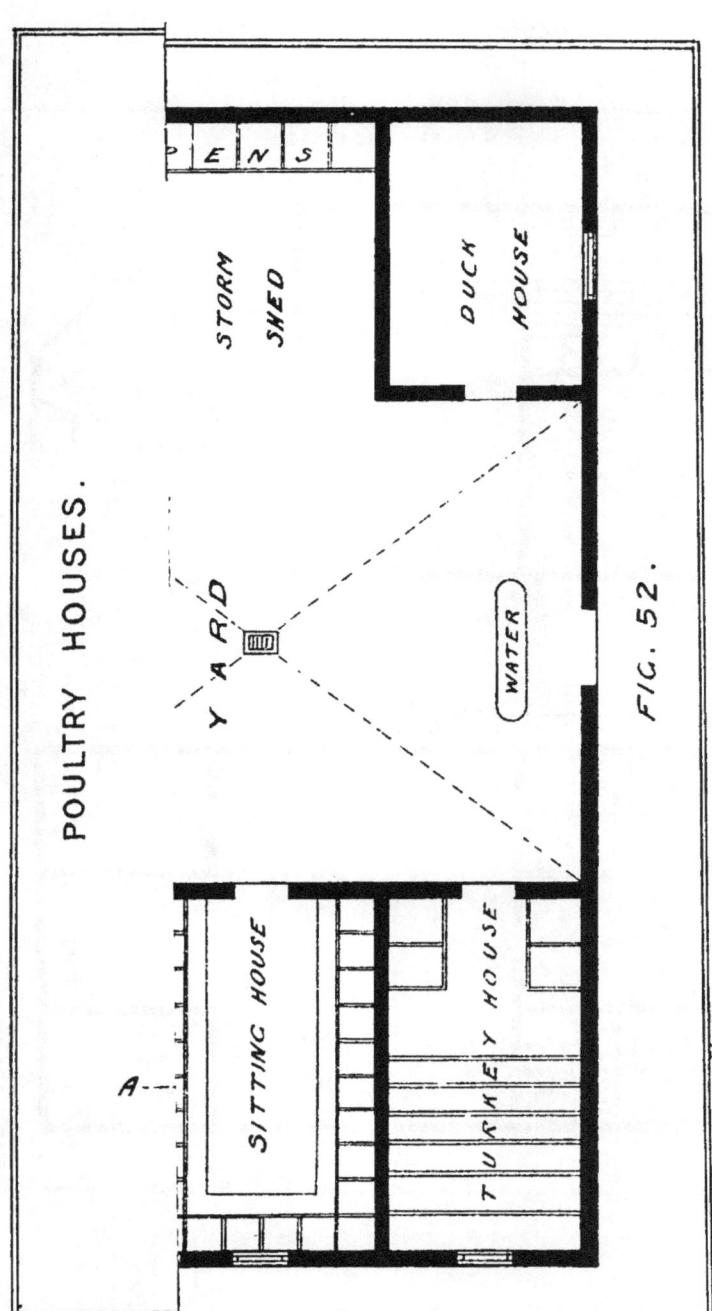

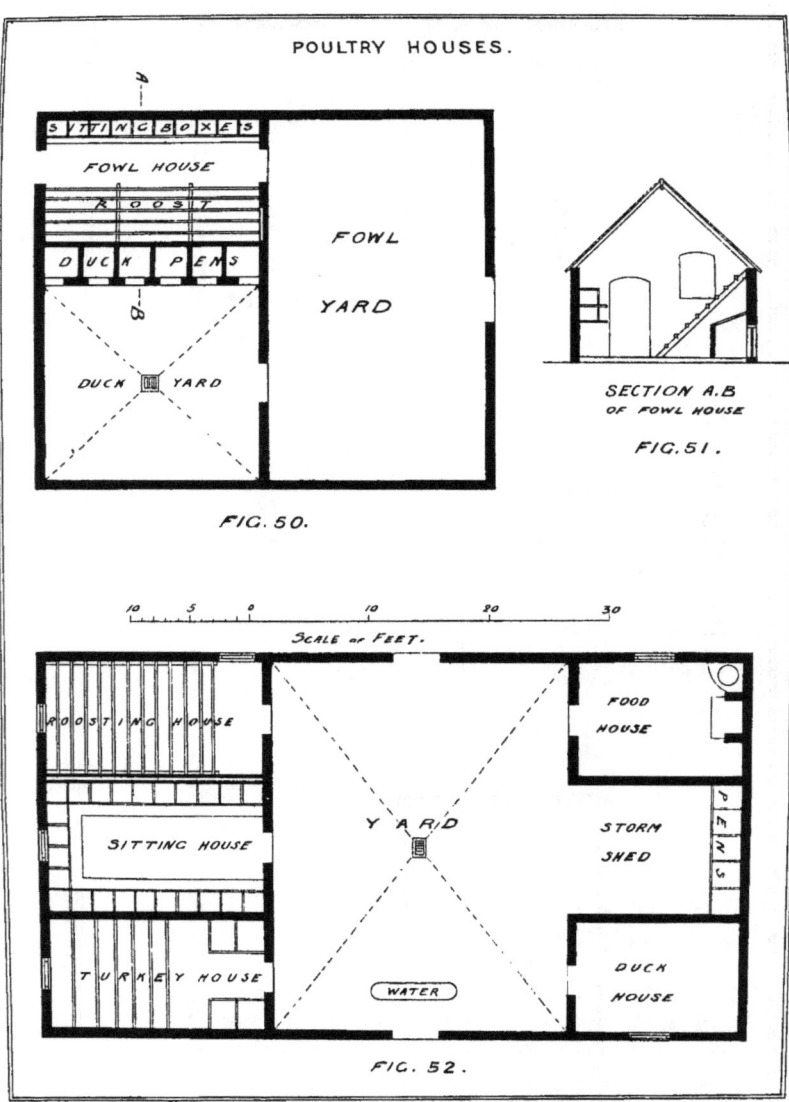

stackyard and a grass paddock is desirable; and the nature of the soil must not be forgotten, as the health of the birds will be affected by undue dampness. Warmth is such an essential element for success and profit, that an effort should be made to secure a sheltered situation and favourable aspect, and if possible a connection with any building possessing a flue, against which the sitting or laying boxes may be placed. The chimney of a piggery boiling-house, or of the engine-house, can sometimes be made use of in this way.

For the purpose of illustration, two plans and a section are given at Figs. 31, 32, and 33. The single house shown in connection with two small yards will be serviceable for general purposes where only one compartment is required. The yards are a useful accompaniment for feeding the fowls and ducks in, and form a secure place for young birds, besides barring the intrusion upon the house of a stray pig or a mischievous dog; and roadways will be kept cleaner and free from the paraphernalia attending the operations of rearing. It will be seen that opening into the duck-yard are six small pens for ducks, formed out of the space of the fowl-house under the roosting perches, and most poultry keepers regard these places as very necessary, as sitting ducks in them are free from molestation and can be securely fastened up at night; or they can be used for geese, and in either case, as the doors communicate with the yard, they can be left open in the daytime without fear of a mishap. It may be said also in favour of these pens that they can be often made to take the place of a separate house costing more to build.

Fig. 33 is a plan intended to meet more extended requirements. A yard here is also given for the use of the poultry, for the reasons before mentioned. Two houses are provided for the fowls, one for roosting and the other for laying and sitting, the latter being in a central situation for the sake of securing greater warmth. A separate house is provided for turkeys, as it is found that in a young state these birds thrive better by themselves. On the opposite side of the yard is a "storm-shed," as it is usually called, with a few small pens at the back for sitting geese and ducks, or shutting up young chickens; and a house for ducks, which are always better apart from the fowls on account of the dirt which they create. There is also a small house for food, with a copper and fireplace, which will be found serviceable where fowls are kept on a large scale.

The principal elements of success in rearing poultry are, as regards building accommodation, warmth, freedom from molestation, and cleanliness. The former has been already mentioned, in recommending the construction of houses where possible adjoining a fireplace flue. A further step in this direction (which the tenant might possibly introduce with advantage at his own cost where his operations are on a large scale) would be the fixing of hot-water or steam pipes in connection with an engine or some other boiler. Freedom from molestation is to be secured in part by fencing off a small enclosure as a yard attached to the houses, but it cannot wholly be attained without building in such a manner as will make it easy to exclude vermin. For this purpose a concrete or well-paved floor is necessary, and in situations where rats are numerous and troublesome, the bottoms of the doors and other woodwork should be covered with zinc or galvanised iron, as these persistent and destructive beasts must be kept away at any cost.

Floors of poultry houses thus constructed are also an advantage in the matter of cleanliness, which is the last but by no means the least of the three elements alluded to as being necessary for success, as they can be swept or washed down occasionally with little trouble. There is no doubt that the troublesome habit of hens laying away is often the result of neglecting to keep fowl-houses and their fittings clean and wholesome, and of the absence of the means of introducing a supply of air to the houses in very hot weather. Fleas are most irritating, and will prevent hens from using a fowl-house, therefore it is desirable to put the laying-boxes together in such a manner that they can be taken to pieces and limewashed, together with all the interior, when necessity arises. This is easily done, and any little attention in this and other respects which may appear necessary will be amply repaid if the fowls are induced to take to the houses and hatch off, where the risks are much less than those attending nests made in a hedgerow or other exposed place. Where nesting-boxes are placed as in the present plans, in tiers at a distance from the ground, a projecting board along each should be fixed so that fowls can alight upon it. and walk along, because from the fact of the nests being covered (as they should be to keep them free from being fouled by droppings) it will be impossible for them to fly up and alight in a position which will enable them to get on to the nests. Roosting perches, as well as other fittings, should be removable, so that the whole interior can be made clear for an occasional thorough limewash out.

The best authorities now agree that roosting perches should be all on one level, about 4 to 5 ft. from the floor, in order to prevent the struggle which goes on to get to the higher ones; and sitting-boxes should be on the floor on account of the beneficial effect of the moisture arising from the ground upon the eggs and the sitting and hatching out.

## CHAPTER XVIII.

#### REPAIRS.

REPAIRS are a constant source of anxiety to land agents, demanding, as they do, a large proportionate outlay on all landed estates ; and as the judgment and skill involved in arranging for their execution is one of the most important matters connected with estate management, a few remarks on the subject may be of service. Since rents have been so materially diminished, the difficulties connected with repairs have been largely increased owing to the want of the necessary funds, and makeshifts have frequently to be resorted to, to minimise the effects of a certain amount of unavoidable neglect.

Customs vary according to locality as to the amount of repairs which are required to be done by the tenants themselves, and in the end, in many instances, it amounts to little or nothing beyond what can be done with rough timber and a few nails ; but whatever arrangements in this respect prevail, it is an agent's duty, as far as lies in his power, to see that all necessary repairs are done when they become apparent. If they are neglected the main fabric will suffer, or general decay will proceed apace, and in the end an increased outlay is needed, out of proportion to the original cost if timely executed.

The question of first importance is as to the best method

of getting the work done, and from an experience of many years I am of opinion that where an estate is of sufficient extent to command the services of a resident agent, or one who can pay fairly frequent visits, it is by far the best course to keep a permanent staff of bricklayers and carpenters at least, if not of other tradesmen, and to let them do the repairs under the most effective supervision obtainable. On comparatively small estates a practical agent, with a foreman for this department selected for his trustworthiness, can see to the work being well and economically done; but on larger properties a competent and careful clerk of works is needed, and a good man of this class is a valuable acquisition, and should receive every encouragement. He will be entrusted with the making of surveys and reports upon such matters as the agent may not have time to take more than a superficial notice of, to keep accurate accounts of stores and men's time, to see that all goods purchased are of satisfactory quality, and that there is an economical administration throughout the whole of his department.

Where an estate staff of permanent workmen is thus kept, all works difficult to estimate for, or measure up, will of course be done by day work; but when a considerable piece of new work has to be undertaken, it is desirable to make piecework of it, and measure it up. It is some encouragement to good men to enable them to increase their earnings somewhat in this way if they are industrious, and advantageous also to the proprietor to be able to check their working speed, and to find out which are the most active workmen. As regards new building of any considerable extent, it is not often, with ordinary repairs on hand, that it can be undertaken by the regular hands as piecework, and in such cases plans and specifications must be drawn up and tenders obtained—from men of known reliability, if possible, by asking these only for estimates.

But it is on properties where, from their small size, permanent tradesmen cannot be kept or properly supervised, or, for similar reasons, on the outlying portions of larger estates, where the difficulty will be most felt in getting repairs done well and economically. It becomes a necessity in such cases either to run up a day-work account, or to get an estimate ; and in either case the result is unsatisfactory, unless an honest and careful builder used to country work can be met with. He is a treasure if obtainable, as he will not put on too much margin of profit, as is often done, to cover the contingencies when giving an estimate for repairs which cannot be measured up, and he will see that a fair day's work is done by his men when no estimate is given. In this part of an agent's work there are many pitfalls, and nothing but experience will enable him to keep entirely clear of them. If he knows the details of his business, or has the assistance of a good clerk of works, it is merely a question of time to become acquainted with such men as can be trusted with the execution of repairs, and when found they must be well looked after. That "knowledge is power" in dealing with such matters is very true, and the man who has learned to "weigh" such work as cannot be measured, after a careful inspection, obtains a considerable advantage for his employer, as by a timely remonstrance or interposition a check is often put upon extravagance in price or materials, or bad workmanship.

It will be of material assistance in dealing with the repairs problem, to prepare and keep at hand a list of prices of the most common class of building works on estates under management. These will vary according to custom or locality, of course, and if tabulated in columns for "labour only" and "all materials" like a much-abridged builder's price-book, they will be useful aids in checking the men's time employed, or of arriving at fair estimates, as well as in determining in the first instance what work shall be done, and the manner of doing it. For instance, if a defective piece of walling or roofing is to be dealt with, it is of service to be able to ascertain readily what it would cost per yard, or per square, to rebuild, or strip and recover, and to compare this with the probable cost of labour if a patching up only was done to the defective parts.

The arrangement with tenants as to repairs will be guided by the customs of the estate, or district, but whatever they may be when submitted in an agreement of tenancy they are often a source of troublesome discussion. It is generally stipulated that a tenant shall keep and leave the premises in good tenantable repair—roofs, main walls, and main timbers, and damage by fire or tempest excepted, which are landlord's liabilities. This is a desirable clause to put in a contract of tenancy, because, notwithstanding the concessions a landlord may make from time to time in executing repairs himself, it protects him against unfair usage by a tenant, if such occurs, by the responsibility attaching to him under his agreement.

But before tenants are willing to sign an agreement with a clause of this kind in, they will generally stipulate that the premises shall be first put in repair by the landlord, and words to this effect can be added; but in all such cases it is good policy for the landlord to do the repairs at the earliest possible opportunity, as little reparations often extend to larger ones under such circumstances. Gates and fences, for instance, often get rapidly worse at such times if not repaired immediately on entry of the tenant.

Of all the troublesome times to listen to requests for repairs, those made on rent audit days are the most disagreeable, and there are a class of tenants who never seem to be able to part with their money without making a grumble and an effort to get something back in the shape of a promise for repairs or improvements. Agents must, of course, give ear to these appeals at some time or other, but if they wish to get through a heavy audit expeditiously they should make it an invariable custom to confine their intercourse with the tenants on rent day to the settlement of rent only, to the exclusion of every other topic, and put up a notice in the waiting-room that they will attend on a certain day, or days, to hear requests or discuss any business matters with the tenants. This has been my practice for many years, and, as a rule, it is cheerfully accepted, as it assists in the rapid despatch of business, and does away with the long and irksome periods of waiting for their turn on the part of the tenants, which would otherwise occur; and one is often comforted by the non-appearance on the appointed day of the habitual grumblers, their requirements after all not being of sufficient importance to necessitate a special visit to the estate office!

In connection with the subject of repairs, a few remarks may be made upon materials, some of which, at least, exist on most landed estates, such as timber, brick earth, limestone, building and paving stone, and sand. These resources should be developed and made use of so far as they can be suitably and economically employed, as they will save the cost of railway and road carriage in remote places.

Carpenters, if left to exercise their own free will, are prone to use foreign timber, because it is easier to work, in preference to home-grown, in places where it is not only unnecessary, but where the other is most suitable. Good deals are of course necessary for joinery work, and they are preferable for many other purposes where a material is required which will not cast. Oak, of course, is not out of place in any farm building work where obtainable; and where there is hard wear, such as with sills for mangers, pigsty doors, and for all kinds of posts, it is necessary for durability. Good larch, or Scotch, perhaps, ranks next for general use in roofs and for boarding, if cut out of sound well-matured trees, but it is of very little service if the timber is small. Poplar is serviceable for rafters and stall boarding, but it must be kept dry; and elm planking and boards are often used for mangers and inside work, but this wood casts, and is otherwise unsuitable for outside weather boarding, except for very rough repairs. Ash is not very suitable for farm building work, but it sells readily always at a good price.

Gate repairs and renewals are a considerable tax upon estate resources, and where oak is obtainable nothing is cheaper or more lasting than good cloven gates. With care they will be serviceable for forty years, outlasting nearly two sawn ones of the same material, and three or four of the light deal gates which are manufactured at some of the timber ports, and which are not worth hanging. It is a good plan to send the cleaver into a wood directly after a fall of oak, and let him select the timber of suitable size and quality for cleaving into gate-bars, pales, ladder and rack staves, and the like, for use on the estate, and let him cleave it on the spot; and if furnished with a sawn head and heel he will cleave and make the gates at from 5s. to 6s. each.

Many estates have their own brickyards, but where this is not the case they can be made in the open fields in the summer-time in "clamps," where suitable earth exists. If a large piece of new building is to be put up, and the bricks can be made in this manner near the job, a great saving in haulage can be effected, but this class of work is not so common as it was formerly.

# APPENDIX.

## MODEL REGULATIONS

### RELATING TO

### DAIRIES, COWSHEDS, AND MILKSHOPS

(*Issued by the Local Government Board*).

(*Draft Form.*)

REGULATIONS MADE BY THE *
WITH RESPECT TO DAIRIES, COWSHEDS, AND MILKSHOPS
IN THE †

### Interpretation.

1. Throughout these Regulations the expression "the Council" means the * ;
the expression "the District" means the † ;
the expression "Cowshed" includes any dairy in which milking cows may be kept; and the expression "Cowkeeper" means any person following the trade of a cowkeeper or dairyman who is, or is required to be, registered under the Dairies, Cowsheds, and Milkshops Order of 1885.

---

\* " Mayor, Aldermen, and Burgesses of the Borough of    , acting by the Council" *or* " Urban (or Rural) District Council of    ," *as the case may be*.

† " Borough " *or* " Urban (*or* Rural) District of    ," *as the case may be*.

### For the Inspection of Cattle in Dairies.

2. Every occupier of a dairy wherein any cattle may be kept, and which the Medical Officer of Health, or the Inspector of Nuisances, or any other officer of the Council specially authorised by them in that behalf, may visit for the purpose of inspecting cattle, and every person for the time being having the care or control of any such dairy, or of any cattle therein, shall afford such Medical Officer of Health, Inspector of Nuisances, or officer, all reasonable assistance that may, for the purpose of the inspection, be required by him.

### For Prescribing and Regulating the Lighting, Ventilation, Cleansing, Drainage, and Water Supply of Cowsheds and Dairies in the occupation of Persons following the Trade of Cowkeepers and Dairymen.

## Part I.

The Regulations in this Part shall apply to cowsheds the cows from which are habitually grazed on grass land during the greater part of the year, and when not so grazed, are habitually turned out during a portion of each day.

### *Lighting.*

3. Every cowkeeper shall provide that every cowshed in his occupation shall be sufficiently lighted with windows, whether in the sides or roof thereof.

### *Ventilation.*

4. Every cowkeeper shall cause every cowshed in his occupation to be sufficiently ventilated, and for this purpose to be provided with a sufficient number of openings into the external air to keep the air in the cowshed in a wholesome condition.

### Cleansing.

5. (1.) Every cowkeeper shall cause every part of the interior of every cowshed in his occupation to be thoroughly cleansed from time to time as often as may be necessary to secure that such cowshed shall be at all times reasonably clean and sweet.

(2.) Such person shall cause the ceiling or interior of the roof and the walls of every cowshed in his occupation to be properly limewashed *twice* at least in every year ; that is to say, once during the month of May and once during the month of October, and at such other times as may be necessary.

Provided that this requirement shall not apply to any part of such ceiling, roof, or walls, that may be properly painted or varnished, or constructed of or covered with any material such as to render the limewashing unsuitable or inexpedient, and that may be otherwise properly cleansed.

(3.) He shall cause the floor of every such cowshed to be thoroughly swept, and all dung and other offensive matter to be removed from such cowshed as often as may be necessary, and not less than *once* in every day.

### Drainage.

6. (1.) Every cowkeeper shall cause the drainage of every cowshed in his occupation to be so arranged that all liquid matter which may fall or be cast upon the floor may be conveyed by a suitable open channel to a drain inlet situate in the open air at a proper distance from any door or window of such cowshed, or to some other suitable place of disposal which is so situate.

(2.) He shall not cause or suffer any inlet to any drain of such cowshed to be within such cowshed.

### Water Supply.

7. (1.) Every cowkeeper shall keep in, or in connection with, every cowshed in his occupation a supply of water suitable and sufficient for all such purposes as may from time to time be reasonably necessary.

(2.) He shall cause any receptacle which may be provided for such water to be emptied and thoroughly cleansed from time to time as often as may be necessary to prevent the pollution of any water that may be stored therein, and where such receptacle is used for the storage only of water, he shall cause it to be properly covered and ventilated, and so placed as to be at all times readily accessible.

## PART II.

The Regulations in Part I., and also the following Regulation, shall apply to all cowsheds other than those the cows from which are habitually grazed on grass land during the greater part of the year, and when not so grazed, are habitually turned out during a portion of each day.

8. A cowkeeper shall not cause or allow any cowshed in his occupation to be occupied by a larger number of cows than will leave not less than *eight hundred feet* of air space for each cow.

Provided as follows :—

(*a.*) In calculating the air space for the purposes of this Regulation, no space shall be reckoned which is more than *sixteen feet* above the floor; but if the roof or ceiling is inclined, then the mean height of the same above the floor may be taken as the height thereof for the purposes of this Regulation.

(*b.*) This Regulation shall not apply to any cowshed constructed and used before the date of these Regulations coming into effect, until two years after that date.

## PART III.

9. In this Part, the expression " Dairy " means a dairy in which cattle are not kept.

### *Lighting.*

10. Every cowkeeper shall provide that every dairy in his occupation shall be sufficiently lighted with windows, whether in the sides or roof thereof.

### Ventilation.

11. Every cowkeeper shall cause every dairy in his occupation to be sufficiently ventilated, and for this purpose to be provided with a sufficient number of openings into the external air to keep the air in the dairy in a wholesome condition.

### Cleansing.

12. (1.) Every cowkeeper shall cause every part of the interior of every dairy in his occupation to be thoroughly cleansed from time to time as often as may be necessary to secure that such dairy shall be at all times reasonably clean and sweet.

(2.) He shall cause the floor of every such dairy to be thoroughly cleansed with water at least *once* in every day.

### Drainage.

13. (1.) Every cowkeeper shall cause the drainage of every dairy in his occupation to be so arranged that all liquid matter which may fall or be cast upon the floor may be conveyed by a suitable open channel to the outside of such dairy, and may there be received in a suitable gully communicating with a proper and sufficient drain.

(2.) He shall not cause or suffer any inlet to any drain of such dairy to be within such dairy.

### Water Supply.

14. (1.) Every cowkeeper shall cause every dairy in his occupation to be provided with an adequate supply of good and wholesome water for the cleansing of such dairy and of any vessels that may be used therein for containing milk, and for all other reasonable and necessary purposes in connection with the use thereof.

(2.) He shall cause every cistern or other receptacle in which any such water may be stored to be properly covered and ventilated, and so placed as to be at all times readily accessible.

(3.) He shall cause every such cistern or receptacle to be emptied and thoroughly cleansed from time to time as often as may be necessary to prevent the pollution of any water that may be stored therein.

**For Securing the Cleanliness of Milk-Stores, Milkshops, and of Milk Vessels used for containing Milk for Sale by Persons following the Trade of Cowkeepers and Dairymen.**

*Cleanliness of Milk-Stores and Milkshops.*

15. Every cowkeeper who is the occupier of a milk-store or milkshop shall cause every part of the interior of such milk-store or milkshop to be thoroughly cleansed from time to time as often as may be necessary to maintain such milk-store or milk-shop in a thorough state of cleanliness.

*Cleanliness of Milk Vessels.*

16. (1.) Every cowkeeper shall from time to time as often as may be necessary cause every milk vessel that may be used by him for containing milk for sale to be thoroughly cleansed with steam or clean boiling water, and shall otherwise take all proper precautions for the maintenance of such milk vessel in a constant state of cleanliness.

(2.) He shall on every occasion when any such vessel shall have been used to contain milk, or shall have been returned to him after having been out of his possession, cause such vessel to be forthwith so cleansed.

**For Prescribing Precautions to be taken by Purveyors of Milk and Persons Selling Milk by Retail against Infection or Contamination.**

17. (1.) Every purveyor of milk or person selling milk by retail shall take all reasonable and proper precautions, in and in connection with the storage and distribution of the milk, and

otherwise, to prevent the exposure of the milk to any infection or contamination.

(2.) He shall not deposit or keep any milk intended for sale—

(a.) In any room or place where it would be liable to become infected or contaminated by impure air, or by any offensive, noxious, or deleterious gas or substance, or by any noxious or injurious emanation, exhalation, or effluvium; or

(b.) In any room used as a kitchen or as a living-room; or

(c.) In any room or building, or part of a building, communicating directly by door, window, or otherwise, with any room used as a sleeping-room, or in which there may be any person suffering from any infectious or contagious disease, or which may have been used by any person suffering from any such disease, and may not have been properly disinfected; or

(d.) In any room or building, or part of a building, in which there may be any direct inlet to any drain.

(3.) He shall not keep milk for sale, or cause or suffer any such milk to be placed, in any vessel, receptacle, or utensil which is not thoroughly clean.

(4.) He shall cause every vessel, receptacle, or utensil used by him for containing milk for sale to be thoroughly cleansed with steam or clean boiling water after it shall have been used, and to be maintained in a constant state of cleanliness.

(5.) He shall not cause or suffer any cow belonging to him or under his care or control to be milked for the purpose of obtaining milk for sale—

(a.) Unless, at the time of milking, the udder and teats of such cow are thoroughly clean; and

(b.) Unless the hands of the person milking such cow also are throroughly clean and free from all infection and contamination.

### Penalties.

18. Every person who shall offend against any of the foregoing Regulations shall be liable for every such offence to a penalty of *five pounds*, and in the case of a continuing offence to a furthe

penalty of *forty shillings* for each day after written notice of the offence from the Council.

Provided, nevertheless, that the justices or Court before whom any complaint may be made, or any proceedings may be taken in respect of any such offence, may, if they think fit, adjudge the payment as a penalty of any sum less than the full amount of the penalty imposed by this Regulation.

### Commencement of the Regulations.

19. These Regulations shall come into force on and after the day of 18 .

### Revocation of Regulations.

20. From and after the date on which these Regulations shall come into force, all Regulations heretofore made under or having effect in pursuance of the Dairies, Cowsheds, and Milkshops Order of 1885, shall, so far as the same are now in force in the district, be revoked.

# INDEX.

## A

ADVANTAGES of proper buildings, 2.
Aids to farming practice, farm buildings as, 4.
Arable farm homesteads, 12, 20, 28.
Arrangement of homesteads, 12.

## B

BARNS, straw, 16, 44.
— Dutch, roofs for, 125-133.
Barns, old, converted to food stores, 34-36.
— converted to two-storey granary, 36.
— converted to other uses, 39.
Blacksmith's shop, 114.
Block system of building, economical, 19.
— economises labour at the homestead, 19.
Boxes for cattle, 72.
Box feeding of cattle, advantages of, 73.
Building improvements, advice on making, 1.
— in a dairy district, 7.
Bull-house, 18.

## C

CAKE-STORES, 45.
Calf-pens, 18.

Calf-pens, construction of, for fattening calves, 68.
— construction of, for rearing calves, 68.
— plans of, 69, 70.
— sparred flooring for, 70.
Cameron, Dr, on the philosophy of sheltering animals, 93.
Carpenter's shop, 114.
Cart-shedding, 17, 112.
— aspect of, 113.
— dimensions of, 112.
— situation of, 112.
— tool-house in connection with, 113.
Chaff-houses, 41, 45, 96.
Climate and locality influences farm building requirements, 25.
Cooking food for pigs, merits of, 111.
Corrugated iron roofing, 12, 125, 133.
— cost of, 13, 89.
— for covered yards, 92.
— for Dutch barns, 125.
Cost of stalls, boxes, and yards with sheds, compared, 73.
Cottages, 157.
— plan and description of pair of, 158, 159.
— cost of erection of, 160.
Covered yards, 83.
— opinions of R.A.S.E. judges on, 83.
— opinions at the Surveyors' Institution on, 84.
— cost of, to reduce, 87.
— ventilation of, 87.
— roofs and roofing material for, 89, 125.

Covered yards, superior value of manure made in, 85.
Cow-houses, 49.
— choice of designs for, 56.
— custom as regards, in different localities, 49.
— dimensions of, 52.
— drain channel for, section of, 60.
— fitting up of, 57.
— mangers for, 64, 65, 66.
— paving, draining, lighting, and ventilation of, 57.
— paving of, with wood, 58.
— plans of double, 54, 55.
— plan of single, 52.
— roof timbers for, 56.
— subject to bye-laws of local authorities, 50.
— stall divisions of, 65, 66.
— window for, 62.
— model regulations of Local Government Board respecting, 51, 183.
Creosoted wood roofs, 125.

## D

DAIRIES, construction of, 163.
— importance of regulating temperature of, 170.
— Messrs Bradford & Co.'s prize plans, 165, 166.
— and milkshops orders, 51.
Dairy farm homesteads, 22, 24.
Drainage of cow-houses, 60.
— homesteads, 14, 116.
— stables, 101.
Drain channel, section of, 60.
Ducks, houses for, 173.
Dunging out, facilities for, in plan, 15.
Dutch barn and other roofing, 125.

## E

EAVES, spouting of, improves manure, 117.
Economical construction described, 21.

Engine-houses, 14, 47.
— for dairies, 167.

## F

FARM buildings, as aids to farming practice, 4.
— considerations affecting the erection of, 2.
Farmhouses, 134.
— altered requirements of, 135.
— size of, how governed, 135.
— site and requirements of, 136.
Farming outlook, 3.
— practice differs, 5.
Feeding boxes for cattle, 72.
— drainage not needed for, 76.
— removing of manure from, facilitated, 74.
— plans and fitting up of, 74, 75, 76.
Feeding stalls for cattle, 72.
— utility and cost of, compared with boxes, open yards, and covered yards, 72.
Fodder-stores, 46.
Fold-yards, open, 12, 18, 34, 77.
— area for each beast in, 82.
— evils of ill-constructed, 77.
— feeding of cattle in, 78.
— fitting up of, 81.
— plan of open yards, 78.
— points and advantages of well-constructed, 80.
— proper dimensions of, 78.
— shelter of, 26, 28.
Fold-yards, covered, 83.
Food department, 41.
Food-stores, 15, 41.
— advantages of, in bad seasons, 41.
— made out of barn, 35.
— plan of, for 400 acres, 44.
Fowl-houses, 16, 172.

## G

GRANARIES, 41, 48.

# Index.

## H

HOMESTEAD, plan of, for 400 acres (R.A.S.E. silver medal design), 12.
— plan of, for 400 acres (from Surveyors' Institution *Transactions*), 20.
— plan of, for dairy farm, 22.
— plan of, for dairy farm of 400 acres, 24.
— plan of, for arable farm of 200 acres, 28.
Homesteads as food manufactories, 2.
— arrangement and general construction of, 10, 12.
— arable, method of alteration for dairy farms, 22, 29.
— improvement of, advice on, 1.
— old, plans of, remodelled, 34, 36.
— old, remodelling of, 31.
— for small holdings, 139.
— plans of houses for, 142, 147, 158, 159.
— plans of homestead for, 148-151.
— specification of homestead for, 150.
Houses for small holdings, 142-147.

## I

INFIRMARY, 16, 115.
Influence of soil, situation, and climate, 6.
Implement shedding, 112.
Importance of facilities for preparing and mixing food, 41.
Iron *versus* wood roofs, 125-133.
— roof, section of curved, 125.
— roof, detailed drawing of, 126.
— roof, materials and cost of, 127.
— roof, flat, on timber, cost of, 131.

## L

LIGHT, cheaply provided in roofs, 13.
Lighting of cow-houses, 61.

Liquid manure, 116.
Local Government Board's Model Regulations respecting cowsheds, 51, 183.
Loft, stable, 96.
Loose boxes, 15, 72.
— for calving cows, 68.

## M

MANGERS for cow-houses, 64, 65, 66.
— for stables, 103.
Manure tanks, suggestions for dispensing with, 116.
— tanks, neglect of use when provided, 116.
Mixing-rooms, 18, 41, 46.
Model Regulations of Local Government Board, 51, 183.

## O

OFFICE for homestead, 16.
Oxfordshire homesteads remodelled, 33.

## P

PAVING of cow-houses, 57.
— of stables, 100.
Pigs, cooking food for, 110.
Pigsties, adapted also for loose boxes, 15.
— box form of sty recommended, 107.
— construction and situation of, 108.
— convenient feeding trough for, 109.
— flooring and drainage of, 108.
— food-house for, and its fitting up, 110.
Poultry-houses, 16, 172.
— plans of, 172.
— rearing, elements of success in, as regards building, 174.

Produce of farms, importance of preparing the, for home consumption, 41.

### R

RACKS for stables, 103.
Rams, hydraulic, 121.
Roof timbers for a wide span, 56.
— of covered yard, 90.
Roof ventilation of covered homestead, 91.
Roofs and roofing material for Dutch barns and covered yards, 92, 125.
Root-houses, 41, 46.
Royal Agricultural Society's recommendations on cow-houses, 51.

### S

SANITARY legislation affecting cow-houses, 50.
Seasons, bad, difficulties of supporting stock in, 41.
Shafting of machinery, 14.
Sheep-sheds, 18.
Shelter-sheds, 28.
— over-mangers, 79.
Slaughter-houses, 16, 115.
Sparred flooring, 70.
Stables, 17, 94.
— dimensions of, 95.
— drainage of, 101.
— fitting up of, 102.
— flooring of, 100.
— hay and chaff store for, 96.
— harness-rooms in, 98.
— high *versus* low racks considered, 103.
— lofts in, 96.
— plans of single and double, 96.
— treatment of horses in, varies in different districts, 94.
- utility of loose boxes attached to, 96.
- ventilation of, 96, 99.
— windows for, 99.

Stalls for cattle, 72
Stock-yards, open, 77.
— covered, 83.
Stores for homestead, 16.
Straw barns, 16, 44.
— stores, 41.
Surveyors' Institution, homestead illustrated in *Transactions* of, 20.
— criticism of members on homestead, 26.
— opinions of members on covered yards, 84.

### T

TOOL-HOUSE, 113.
Tuberculosis and cow-houses, 51.
Turkeys, house for, 174.

### V

VENTILATING shafts under mangers, 13.
Ventilation, 13.
— of dairies, 168.
— of covered yards, 87.
— of cow-houses, 61.
— of stables, 14.

### W

WARMTH, beneficial effects of, 50.
Water supply, 14, 119.
— importance of pure, for dairy purposes, 120.
Windmills for pumping, 122.
Windows for farm buildings, 61.
Winnowing floor, 17, 48.
Wood paving for cow-houses, 58.
— *versus* iron roofs, 125, 133.
— roofs, section of, 124.
— specification of, 129.
— cost of, 130.

### Y

YARDS, open, 12, 18, 77.
— covered, 83.

www.ingramcontent.com/pod-product-compliance
Lightning Source LLC
Chambersburg PA
CBHW032041150426
43194CB00006B/369